A Tramper's Journey

Stories from the Back Country of New Zealand

Mark Pickering

CRAIG
POTTON
PUBLISHING

To the keen trampers who keep the hills alive, and to my daughter
Alex and partner Rachel, who keep me lively.

First published in 2004 by Craig Potton Publishing
98 Vickerman Street, PO Box 555, Nelson, New Zealand
www.craigpotton.co.nz

© Photography: Mark Pickering and individual photographers
©Text: Mark Pickering

ISBN 1-877333-17-4

Editing by James Brown
Cover design by Kris Sowersby
Printed in China by Everbest Printing Co. Ltd

Contents

Foreword

It was a long time ago, when New Zealand was still at the end of the world. A man carried his swag across the dry Mackenzie country, sweating in the late spring heat and dossed down for the night at Haldon Station. Station owners were usually fairly obliging to these itinerant men, often giving them a feed as well as a bed, and on any day of the week, a back-country sheep station like Haldon might get four or five men a night, travelling off the hot plains and peering into the cookhouse just on sundown.

This particular evening was quiet. The owner of Haldon Station at that time was Thomas Teschemaker who kept a diary, and the entry for 12 October 1866 noted curtly, 'A tramper slept here...'

This is one of the earliest literary references to the word 'tramper'. Tramping (a uniquely New Zealand term for hiking or bushwalking) started in New Zealand as a necessity, the end result of a long process of human engagement with the mountains, and the tramping culture that we have inherited is a direct descendant of the difficult geography and travelling privations that the first back-country travellers had to endure. They left behind an infrastructure and an attitude.

Going back even further, we unknowingly follow Maori trails several hundred years after the passage of war parties and family groups, and we use tuwhana, the Maori pole technique for crossing rivers safely. The early European explorers 'discovered' the land again, and although they used blankets instead of down sleeping bags, and oilskins instead of Goretex, they were trampers just the same—wading rivers, bashing through wet bush, hobbling over passes, and yarning at campfires with the aromatic flavour of woodsmoke in their billy tea.

Working-class colonists tramped their cheap labour into the high country, and station owners constructed huts for the lonely boundary keepers and rabbiters. In the back country there are still at least 30 huts

Early morning on the Trent River flats, West Coast.

that are over 100 years old. Governments built pack tracks for gold diggers and huts for deer cullers, and modern day trampers and hunters utilise these by right.

This book is about celebrating tramping: a persistent part of New Zealand's culture and a legacy of an empty country covered with empty mountains. But trampers have been shy with their stories, and I was puzzled (and still am) by the absence of tramping stories on bookshelves. Hunters have been spinning yarns for years, and the whole gamut of hunting has been recorded in many fine stories. Fisherfolk's perennial fishy tales are well catered for, high-country farmers tell their tales, climbers have had a few distinguished autobiographies written, but trampers have remained mostly silent.

So this book attempts to fill the gap a little with a personal view of tramping, loosely structured around three decades of tramping journeys and experiences, interwoven with observational essays and hut logbook extracts. I also persuaded some friends to add their stories as well. Most of the adventures are small scale, and I have tried to tell inclusive stories that will bring back memories for people, and fire them up to head out into the hills again.

A surprising source of inspiration were the old hut logbooks I came across in the National Archives. I could still smell the woodsmoke as I opened the pages, and see the smudges of black billies and even crushed sandflies. There was my own name, and the names of some of my friends, scrawled in haste 20 years or more ago.

Lastly, I drew upon my own journals. Someone, it might have been Brian Hunt, a Wellington tramper, told me to keep a journal of tramping trips—'you'll never regret it, sunshine'—and he was right! Often neglected, but always brought up-to-date, the journals turned out to be an accurate and evocative record of half a lifetime spent in the hills.

The period covered by this book is roughly between 1974 and 2004, 30 years all told, from tramping club days in Wellington, to forays into the tramping heartland of the Southern Alps. Some material has come from articles I wrote over the years for newspapers and magazines, but most of the stories have never been published before. They are all true—well, most of them.

CHAPTER ONE

BILLY AND PACK

Club Tramping in the 1970s

If you stand on Lambton Quay
On Friday night then you will see
In rain and snow the trampers go
To the Tararua Ranges.

Away, away with billy and pack
A-rollicking down the mountain track
We'll all get lost and never come back
In the Tararua Ranges.

I t seems like a dream, a dream where the colours are different. The blues look bluer and the greens stronger. The young men had shoulder length hair and straggly beards, the women looked plump and burnt. They sang songs around the camp-fire, mostly Irish folk songs, or locally written songs about the Tararuas, and every club had its own songbook. *No More Double-Bunking, A Fast Pair of Skis, In the Tararua Ranges,* and perhaps a few Beatles or Elton John songs would creep in. The camp-fires burned huge and wastefully, the embers flying off into the dark starlight hotels of long ago.

The Greeks have a word for it: 'nostalgia', a certain mixture of remembrance and longing, a feeling of innocence lost, of happiness that had a joyful, uncertain, spontaneous freedom.

In the hills I found friendship and meaning, and in an accidental fashion, explored the back country of New Zealand and every quirky rural road that had a 'No Exit' sign at the beginning and possibilities at the end. I experienced rain on the fly sheet, muddy swollen rivers where you couldn't see your feet, clear frozen dawns, nights of top and tailing and sometimes bush solitude, though club tramping was hardly a lonely business. With parties of, on average, 12 to 20 people, we bustled along the muddy tracks, set up massive fly camps and rearranged the wilderness furniture to suit our needs. We must have scared off every bird for miles and trampled through the delicate forest ecosystem with a benign bumbling ignorance.

We are more sensitive now, more concerned. We worry over burning firewood, drink our water with a certain suspicion about the lurgies inside it, and get mad over the possum damage. The mountains that once seemed so robust when I was a young tramper now seem threatened on all sides by introduced pests, pollution and endless tourist demands. It's not quite as simple as that—perhaps it never was. The mountains have not lost their simplicity, but we've got more complicated.

A sunny day in the Tararuas.

Tongue and Meats

The Wellington Tramping and Mountaineering Club (WT & MC) was the young man's choice of club in the city, with about 400 members. They proudly knew themselves as the 'Tongue and Meats', apparently because when the club started up (in 1947, I believe) they shared the same initials as the 'Wellington Tongue and Meat Company'. I joined the club for my first ever tramping trip in December 1974, hoping matters would go smoothly, and indeed there were some vivid and novel moments.

We were halfway up the Rimutaka Hill when the bus engine seized. Being English and sensible, and newly in the country, I thought, 'Oh well, that's it, we will have to go home now.' However, this obvious line of behaviour did not occur to anyone else. Instead, the driver threw his cigarette away in disgust, laconically muttered something about 'getting another one', and hitched off down the hill into the gathering dusk.

I couldn't quite believe it: would he come back? The trampers on the bus started playing soccer on the road with a tin can while an hour ticked by. Friday night cars swept past us in a blaze of headlights and hurried on up the hill, and then, after two hours, a low throttled roar announced that another Runciman bus was indeed coming to our rescue. Packs were thrown into the new bus, and we were off again without a thought to the bus parked halfway up the hill.

I was bewildered by the twists and turns leading to the Mangatainoka road end (a word I couldn't get my English-trained tongue around) where packs were unloaded in what I later came to understand was a characteristic shambles of noise and shouting. Everyone seemed to know where to go except me. Torches flashed, trip leaders bellowed and different tramping parties took off in a thousand different directions. The bus roared off and suddenly I was alone, or at least it felt like it.

There was one other bloke left behind, adjusting his straps. He looked at me curiously, as if I had just come from Mars. The following conversation took place.

'I'm on the Easy Trip.'

'Oh yeah?'

'Are you?'

'Nope.'

He adjusted another buckle interminably. I heard my first morepork. Then he showed clear and alarming signs of leaving. I had to ask the question I was dreading.

'Do you know where the Easy Trip is?'

'Nope.'

Off to the hills! Probably the Ruahines (1975).

He slung on his pack. He volunteered a comment.

'Lost 'em 'ave yer?'

'Yes.'

Humiliated, I had to admit it. Two minutes off the bus and I'd 'lost 'em'. He volunteered another comment.

'Probably that way.'

'Where?'

'Over the bridge.'

'What bridge?'

He nodded vaguely and I made out some torches dangling over a black void. So that's where everyone had gone! I almost panicked, and in my haste to catch up and get across my first swingbridge, at night, the borrowed pack got caught up in the wires.

At the other side I met up with the trip leader, Ian Bunckenburg, who 'wondered where I'd got to', and we plunged up a bush track to some trees where people were flinging down their sleeping bags and someone was pumping a primus like fury. I hadn't brought a sleeping mat, so I banked up my pitiful bits of clothes, huddled into my borrowed sleeping bag, and froze. The stars were cold and had no charm that night. Nobody spoke to me. I felt miserable.

But the morning brought compensations—a sunny day and bacon sizzling on a primus. Two other groups of trampers disappeared and the Easy Trip that I'd signed up for took on human names and faces.

Every event that day was a first. I felt most peculiar in my shorts, nice natty corduroys, and even stranger sloshing up a river without even taking my boots and socks off. There was even an odd introspective charm about watching my first sandfly burrow happily into my skin. We sweated up to Cattle Ridge Hut and gazed at the views, then swam in the Ruamahanga River and set up camp beside it, building a huge cathedral of flame. There were stars again, friendly this time, and girls, also friendly, and sitting around an argumentative camp-fire was a totally unexpected form of bliss.

I got sunburn, nappy rash, and fell in love. I was sold.

Six years earlier in England in January 1969, at the age of fifteen, I had signed an impressive piece of paper with a large red seal and became an Indentured Apprentice Compositor. The art of 'composing' is the finicky placement of minute individual pieces of type, set upside down in a tool called a 'composing stick'. Other lines were added then spaced with 'leads', tied up with 'page cord' and 'proofed' on a hand press. Once the text had been checked by a proofreader and corrections made, the business card or letterhead was locked into a 'chase' using 'quoins' and 'furniture', and sent to the machine minder for printing. Afterwards the type came back, sticky with printing ink, to be cleaned and 'dissed' (distributed) back into the type cases. This is pretty much what I did for five and a half years, with extensive stints learning to use the Intertype line composing machine as well.

At the end of my apprenticeship I was a fully qualified 'journeyman', which I interpreted rather literally. In 1974 it was easy and commendable for journeymen printers to emigrate anywhere in the English speaking world: Australia, New Zealand, Canada, South Africa, even Kenya all had advertised vacancies in the so-called 'printers' paper' of the day, *The Daily Mail*. It was simple: you saw a doctor, paid £25 in cash, and for two years a job was guaranteed for you on the other side of the world. All expenses were paid by the host government, and they even threw in permanent residency as well. When I arrived in New Zealand the official unemployment rate was nil, with some 300 or so 'special workers', but within three months the Norman Kirk Labour government imposed new restrictions on immigration. By luck, I had just snuck in.

I have often marvelled at the relative artlessness that made me choose New Zealand. I chose quite blindly, in fact on the basis of nothing at all. I wanted to escape from grey England, I wanted to travel, I wanted freedom from my parents. I had never heard of tramping, in fact I'm not reliably sure I even knew if New Zealand had mountains. But I soon found out.

The Tararua Range was the WT & MC's tramping 'playground', a convoluted chain of 1500 metre mountains. The tops are very decent material if you can see where you're going, and that's the problem. The weather is abominable. Official weather statistics reveal that the tops are covered with rain or cloud or both for 80 per cent of the time, and in my own trip journals I recorded that it rained on 75 per cent of the tramps.

Like the song, for each tramp we gathered on Friday nights down by the Railway Station at Jervois Quay (not Lambton Quay), usually at seven o'clock, but six o'clock for the Ruahine Ranges or Tongariro National Park.

The WT & MC divided trips into four categories: Easy, up to three hours a day; Medium, up to six hours a day; Fit, up to eight hours; and Fitness Essential, over eight hours. I mostly stuck to Ms and Fs, and found the FEs a trifle daunting. People were often classified by their fitness, so you might refer to so-and-so as an 'FE', usually some physical brute of a man who bestrode the club room like a colossus and wore shorts all through Wellington's winter. One of these demi-gods wore leather shorts all winter.

The club had a transport arrangement with a bus company called Runciman Motors, in the Hutt Valley, and the owner supplied old dunger buses and similar drivers. Transport costs were cheap and subsidised by the club, and varied according to the distance to the (usually Tararua) road end. The closest was Smith Creek at $2 a head (remember these are 1975 prices I'm talking about, milk was still four cents a bottle!), the furthest at Mangatainoka River was $3.75. With my food costing about $4, I could do a weekend trip and still afford a taxi home on Sunday night ($2). So all-up for a weekend the cost was under $10. To put it in perspective, I was paying $9 a week for rent, $6 for food and taking home about $65 a week from my job as a compositor in the printing factory.

Most of the tramping gear we treasured then, now looks rather quaint and inadequate, which in fact it was. Cheap woollen tops were bought from the Salvation Army for a couple of dollars, and we also got our long johns from the same source, averting eyes away from the obvious stains. Bush shirts were big, baggy and universal, and parkas were usually japara, a black oilskin that faded to white if you had owned it too long. The new-fangled plastic Line 7 parkas were just coming in; they were heavy, sweaty, tough and bright, just the thing for bashing through Tararua scrub.

Boots were heavy, with screwed-in soles and a zillion internal screws which would slowly work their way through into your feet. Some people had tricounies attached to their boots, which were metal clips designed to give you a grip on logs, and I suppose were a replacement for hobnailed boots.

Packs were steel or aluminium 'H-frames', with a cube of canvas attached. There were still some original wooden frame 'Trapper Nelsons' about, but the popular models were 'Mountain Mules', and I still have my 'Super Expedition' version. It was absolutely the latest thing, an alu-

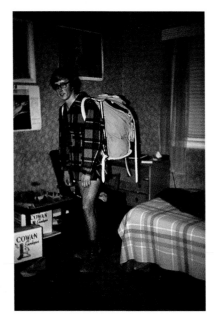

Ready for the hills with my first pack, a Hallmark Everest (1975).

15

minium U-frame supporting a pack of heavy-duty canvas, which still didn't keep the rats out.

At Cone Flat one frosty morning a tramper next to me in the tent pulled out a loaf of Vogel bread for his breakfast to find that overnight the rats had eaten his loaf completely hollow. He swore loudly a few times, drawing very public attention to his annoyance. Then it suddenly dawned on him to check his pack. The rats had gnawed right through the heavy canvas to get at the bread even though he'd been using the pack as a pillow.

Sleeping bags were universally known as 'the pit' and to go to sleep was 'to hit the pit'. They were filled with down (synthetic fibre bags hadn't come in yet), though one or two people still had old kapok bags, which were extremely heavy. 'Poofter pads', 'snowfoam' and 'pixie pads' were all names for a closed-cell foam mat that we used as passable mattresses. They were folded and stuffed down the back of the packs.

Were the packs heavy? Of course they bloody were, although that was due more to the implements inside. We just seemed to carry more stuff then.

As part of the 'party gear', we always carried an axe, and we used it. Club tramping was a licence for pyromaniacs and we took full advantage of the opportunity. One tramping party was getting a lunch brew going beside a log jam in a creek, and then shortly discovered they'd set the whole works alight. What was supposed to be a 40-minute lunch break turned into a three-hour fire alert as they scampered around futilely trying to dowse the flames with billies of water. In the end they managed to shift some boulders in the stream and redirect it into the base of the beast to tame it.

Club tents were the standard four person 'A' shape with a sewn-in floor or 'rain trap', for once water was inside it would run around on the floor oozing into everybody. These tents were not wind resistant, and on stormy nights on the tops someone, usually the one who felt the most worried, would constantly have to get out and re-tie the guy ropes that had slackened off in the wind. At worst, you had to hang onto the poles themselves, and on one wild night near Mt Ruapae I saw an aluminium tent pole bend in the hands of a man who was trying very hard to stop it bending.

Most groups took flys, and these were more comfortable and practical. Huge square sheets of nylon, reinforced with cords at the corners and along the edges, and tied between two trees, they took four people comfortably, five easily, and six at a squeeze. They were social and open and a little cold perhaps, but the wind kept them dry, and when the morning sun came you could throw over a flap and relax like an Italian diva on her sun-drenched terrace.

I started to lead trips in mid-1975 with a zeal that was at times misplaced. It was the leader's job to get the morning brew for the troops, though they always grumbled. One morning at the Ohau River road end I could see it getting lighter in the east, and fiddled about with the primus to boil the billy. By this time I'd woken the other two in the fly, so I shoved a hot bowl of tea in their faces and trudged across the wet paddock to the other fly and woke them up with a loud 'brew's up!'

There was silence, and then someone rustled.

'Eh?'

'Here's your tea, you slugs.'

'What time is it?'

'Time to get going.'

There was a silence as this was digested.

'I know this is a fit trip, but isn't this a bit early?'

'Well, we've gotta get going.'

'At two in the morning?'

Just then the full moon rose, shining benevolently on my embarrassment, and the worst of it was I had to repeat the whole performance again at seven.

Ahh, Tararua tramping, there are so many things I haven't talked about. Floating on car inner tubes down the groin-gripping cold of the Waiohine River, and without the luxury of wetsuits. Thrashing along on a leatherwood ridge, where the only water to be found was in a

Medium tramps were the most popular category in club tramping. 1975 WT & MC tramping trip in Egmont National Park on a three-day weekend, 28 people, and just look at those packs.

deer wallow, so you had to get down on your belly and carefully suck it out using a tarn tube. Crossing endless brown, mucky, dirty, swollen creeks. Stripping off and sunbathing on Totara Flats when the toetoe is unmoving in the heat. Walking along the narrow ridge of the Broken Axe Pinnacles in the weird fellowship of Brocken Spectres, your own gigantic shadows cast on the clouds below. Navigating along the Dundas Ridge and peering hopefully at the compass as someone queries in a helpful but anxious tone, 'The red end does point north, doesn't it?'

It was a training ground, both physical and mental. I've done my best to explain why we persisted, but it's unexplainable. Tararua pride or Tararua bloody-mindedness? A friend of mine has tramped *thirteen* Southern Crossings and has never seen the view from Mt Hector. We've all gone on to much better and (let's be honest) much nicer mountains, but it seems that if you could squeeze an iota of enjoyment out of the mud-dolloped, sour, misbegotten Tararua hills, you could get pleasure anywhere.

No one is proud to admit they've got lost, but it happens to just about everyone. Of course, there are degrees: wandering around for an hour or so in freezing fog on a tussock hill or trying to find the right bush spur down are merely frustrating. Walking off a track happens all the time, but it only becomes a problem when you don't realise it, as the following story reveals.

On my first bushcraft course in 1975 we had walked in by the Smith Creek track to the Tauherenikau flats. On Sunday afternoon, after the traditional and glorious water fight, the 60 or so bushcrafters (we had two buses, an important point to remember) slowly packed up and drifted away. There was much talk of Joe's track.

I did not know it then, but Joe was Joe Gibbs, who had helped build Field Hut, and lived in Tauherenikau Hut, which he had built in 1930. He lived in it well into his seventies and had his eightieth birthday there. The hut burnt down in 1972. Joe's track was an unmarked short cut from Smith Creek up a spur onto the Marchant Ridge track, which he must have used regularly.

Joe's track was known to be quicker and better suited for the faster trampers or 'guns'. Now, I could hardly count myself a 'gun', but I wanted to. The slower trampers had gone ahead and I was somewhere in the middle on my own. I knew the turn-off to the track at least, and when I got there, rather than wait, I carried on. My 'track' was little more than a worn trail, which quickly became more obscure as I followed it up.

Now I was on deer trails, and then nothing much at all. It was getting harder and slower. I waited for the others. No one came. I yelled out hopefully, but there was no answer. So I pushed on, struggling in some horrible scrub as I slowly and obscenely made my way up onto Marchant Ridge. By now, I realised I had missed the track and was in danger of missing the bus. I was worried, not only about delaying the rest of the party, but making such a public fool of myself. What would the Chief Guide say?

The last bit of scrub was the toughest, and I had to crawl underneath gorse and manuka before I burst out onto the Marchant track in a half-crazed panic. It was quarter to five. The buses left at five. I'd have to motor all right, and I did. I raced down Puffer Track just in time to see the two buses in the distance going down the Kaitoke Road.

They hadn't waited for me. I couldn't believe it. No search parties? Perhaps they were going to get the police? All kinds of wild thoughts raced through my mind. I persuaded an old couple to give me a lift to the Upper Hutt railway station, where I got a train to Wellington and a taxi home.

The first thing I did was ring the Chief Guide (I shall spare his blushes and name), who was the lead instructor on the bushcraft course, and breathlessly reassure him.

'It's OK. I've got out all right.'

'Eh?'

'I missed the bus.'

'Eh?'

'Didn't you know?'

'Eh?'

He didn't. There had been a cursory check of the numbers on board, but with two buses everyone assumed I was on the other bus. Besides, only a few people knew me, and what was one tramper lost?

Ill Met by Moonlight

Tramping at night is largely a Wellington club peculiarity, and the logic of it is implacable. People had only a weekend for their trip, so in order to reach the deepest and hardest parts of the range they had to stretch the daylight boundaries into the hours of darkness. Most trips graded 'fit' would require at least two to three hours of night tramping. For example, the well-known Southern Crossing meant that you were expected to walk up to Field Hut on Friday night.

The bus left town at five and got to the road end by seven. Because the large buses the WT & MC hired could not go down the narrow Otaki Forks road, you had to tramp one and a half hours just to get to Otaki Forks. Then it was a three hour slog up to Field Hut, so maybe you'd hit the pit by midnight. If you were on an FE trip, you would continue on to Kime Hut, another two hours or so before you were allowed a little sleep. That's six and a half hours walking on a Friday night, and you'd get to bed at one or two in the morning. These poor sods were usually doing what was called a 'Southern Main Range', from Kime Hut to Mangahuka and Anderson Hut, and back through Waitewaewae, a 35-kilometre round trip involving almost 3000 vertical metres of climbing and over ten peaks—in a weekend!

On my first night tramp (my fourth tramp ever) in 1975 I got myself into a complete mess. We were going up to Mountain House, an old club hut on the ridge to Mt Holdsworth. Although the Gentle Annie track was not the well-graded garden path it is now, it was still only about one and a half hours up to the hut. From there fit parties could launch over Mt Holdsworth to Mid Waiohine, or along to Angle Knob and McGregor, or down to Totara Flats and on to Cone Hut for the weekend.

I was not fast enough for the quick ones and fell behind, but I was still going too fast for the plodders and the trip leader. My torch was inadequate and I was now on my own. My pride kept me going, though I knew nothing about the track apart from what I saw on my large scale map, which usefully included parts of the Wairarapa coast. It started to drizzle. I went past the junction to Totara Flats and started to look for the second side-track to Mountain House. I'd been told about it, but didn't have a clue where it was. Was that it? My torch fell on a black stump. Or there? A small gap in the bush had become a highway. It was getting late and getting dark, and my torch was getting dimmer.

Obviously I had missed the side-track because after a while I found myself sloughing through shin-deep mud with scrub on either side. As I struggled to get out my map, I dropped my torch in the mud. I swore. The torch went out, and indeed decided on a permanent holiday. I swore again and looked around fearfully. Probably I should wait, but it was cold in the rain, and the others might take the side-track and miss me and I'd be there all night. That would be embarrassing, I certainly couldn't risk that. I was just about to walk back when someone else walked right into me and jabbed the barrel of a gun into my stomach and said, 'Bugger.'

I dropped my map in surprise.

He turned out to be a hunter, with his brother. His torch had gone and his brother's torch had the strength of a desiccated glow-worm. They were also wandering around the quagmire of Pig Flat (we decided we were on Pig Flat) looking for the side-track. While I scrabbled in the mud for my map, our desultory conversation revealed that none of us had been to effing Mountain House before, or knew the effing track, and we wished it would stop effing raining. Eventually, for want of a better plan and knowing the hut must be very close, we decided to blunder on, and in true tramping tradition two minutes later we stumbled upon the side-track which led to the hut and candles welcomely glowing through the thick dark night.

Night tramping is an acquired taste, and I don't think I ever acquired it. Normal objects become sinister shadows, roots trip you up, branches strike your face and the tramp becomes an ill-tempered slog. Indeed, some evening trips up rivers were nightmares: stumbling over boulders, getting half soaked in an ice-cold river pool and arriving wet and exhausted at a totally full hut, you wondered why you did it. Perhaps it was part of the tramping culture, and reaching a hut at midnight was some sort of notch on your manly autobiography to date.

There were, however, special evenings when the full moon turned the bush leaves into points of luminescence and light clouds scurried like skittish Titanias eluding a plodding Oberon; and nights when the air was warm yet clear, a rare combination in the Tararua mountains where warmth often meant wet.

On one midsummer's eve on the climb up to Field Hut I was taking a breather, my legs sprawled out across the track, some trampers in our party way ahead, some way behind. The starlight was so bright I had switched off my torch and was listening to a morepork's gentle lament. A solitary woman tramper from our party approached, head down, circumspectly following the point of her torch beam. She started to negotiate her patient way over yet more logs, when she suddenly realised that these 'logs' were different. They were soft, white and yielding—my legs in fact. Two people had their blood curdled by the scream that night.

Christmas in the Hills

There's nothing quite like completely new country. Sooner or later, no matter how much you yearn for the Tararua Ranges, and fondly long for the slosh of mud on your shins up Fields Track or the invigorating bite of the cold Waitewaewae River around your groin, you're going to have to get a life and head south. Across the ditch lie the Southern Alps—the massive chain of mountains that starts practically at Picton and ends in the nemesis, as we thought of it, that is Fiordland.

It's both a physical and psychological lure. The North Island simply cannot compete with the myths of the Arawhata River or the romance of the Garden of Eden. Wellington trampers hear these names and cannot resist the call, or else they pack it all in and become career bureaucrats.

For a couple of years I'd been hearing stories of the 'Christmas Trips' down into the South Island to places I'd never heard of, yet which seemed to roll off the tongue of my imagination. The Olivines, the Red Hills, the Matukituki, Landsborough, Arawhata—the names alone whetted my appetite, and I pored over maps, studying these fantastic regions and desperately wanting to go, but first I had to be asked.

Usually Christmas trips were organised in two-week packages, allowing a day either side for travel. That left about fourteen days for tramping. Now it would be pretty hard to carry fourteen days of food first up. Some trips did it, but you were talking of 30- or even 40-kilogram packs. You can't walk very far with that sort of load, particularly if you're bush-bashing up a hill on the first day. So most WT & MC Christmas tramps had an air-drop placed somewhere.

Not only did the air-drop relieve considerable pressure from a tramper's back, but it added a touch of romance to the expedition, and a few goodies (like sherry, Christmas puds and medicinal brandy) were slipped in to spice up the occasion. The drops were usually at the half-way point of the tramp, and the charm of having (relatively) unlimited amounts to eat and swigging back a mouthful of sherry under the starlight hotel of the Red Hills is as memorable experience as you could wish for.

In the bad old days food drops were quite literally *dropped*, pushed out of a moving aircraft, and you hoped the cartons bounced. In these situations the food was packed in large straw-stuffed wooden boxes, with a vague idea that the straw and timber would absorb some of the impact. It was, rather literally, a hit and miss affair. The pilot brought his mate along to shove the stuff out, and he only had one chance to get it right. Too early and it could be in a river; too late and it missed the river flat and smashed its way through the bush canopy; too high and the contents would explode in a spectacular fashion—normally quite robust tins splitting open and leaving their mangled contents scrambled across the landscape for the keas to pick over.

This sort of result did not impress the tramping party, who turned up three weeks later and were lucky to salvage a tin of beans. The straw carried seeds which could infect the remote landscape with all sorts of interesting weeds, and I've seen remote mountain flats littered with thistles, dock and couch grass. After several of these debacles, tramping leaders insisted that the planes *landed*, and, failing that, hired helicopters. But even then no system was entirely foolproof.

Sometimes the weather turned crook and the pilot couldn't get in at all. I heard one story of a tramping party arriving in bad weather at their food drop at Williamson Flat on the Arawhata River to find nothing, despite endlessly scouring the flat. The next day was a bit better but with low cloud, and they heard a plane buzzing around and guessed it was their provisions circling in an attempt to find a hole in the cloud. They went on to half rations, soup and rice, and gloomily considered the prospect of tramping six days on one Tararua biscuit a day. The second day brought the plane back again, but also the blanket of cloud, and after a fruitless search for a gap the plane droned away again.

Realising that it might be clearer down the valley, they raced to the next flat, McArthur, but there was still no food. So the next day they reluctantly retraced their steps to the first drop off, and just as they got there a plane emerged from the dark cloud, made a high circle about 150 metres up, and released several little black objects which descended with alarming venom to the ground. The cartons had been designed to be dropped from about 60 metres, so you can imagine the impact (as the leader bitterly remarked, 'fireworks without the sparks'), and the party spent a good day retrieving bits and pieces of dried food from over a wide area of river flat. The Christmas whisky was smashed and the white spirits had spoiled half the rice. They never did find the Christmas puddings.

The food for a Christmas tramp was very carefully planned, and it had to be. For a two-week tramp you do not have the luxury of chucking in a few things just before you leave. All food—breakfasts, lunches, dinners, even sweets—was organised and rationed. Five lollies and half a bar of chocolate a day; three Tararua biscuits for lunch; one slice of salami; one small wedge of cheese; a spread of jam, marmite or peanut butter, but *no* mixing of spreads, thank you very much. You could have butter and marmite, but not butter, marmite *and* jam. I have seen people almost come to blows over such issues.

Tararua biscuits are a simple concoction of oats, honey, flour and butter baked hard. The principle was that they were filling and that they should stay in one piece. Bread quickly disintegrated inside the cement mixer of a pack, and crackers were no better. Tararua biscuits became a sort of legend in their time, and it was impossible to think of going on a Christmas tramp without them. Everyone had their own recipes, some of which were less successful than others. Often you would not find out if your biscuits were up to the mark until you were halfway up the Arawhata River and unable to rectify any shortcomings. This tended to mean that the amateur cooks, whose job it was to make the bickies, tended to veer towards baking them hard, rather than risking them falling apart. A soft Tararua biscuit was deeply humiliating. Some were monsters of concrete (and even iron reinforcing, it was suspected), and only a period of flotation in a bowl of hot tea would get them to yield their culinary goodness. We chewed, we gnawed, we even sucked.

The butter and cheese came in tins especially bought by the club from export products that usually went to India. Porridge was allocated at 75 grams per person per day, rice at 50 grams per person per day. If that sounds rather small, it *was* rather small, and for the first few days you felt hungry, no doubt about it, but later as your stomach shrank, your body adjusted to the tight rations and responded well. Any flab

Cooling down at a tarn on Mt Raddle. (Photo: Mike Hollis)

27

you had going in was quickly eliminated, and most trampers ended their trips tanned, fresh and fit. However, on 'pit days' or 'rest days' when there was little else to do except drink endless bowls of billy tea, food was an incessant talking point, from about day two onwards.

I still have my old ration book from when I organised Christmas tramp food. Breakfasts might be porridge and sultanas, or rice and apples—or sometimes a curried rice. Lunches were always Tararua biscuits; and dinners would typically be macaroni cheese, rice and bacon (about the only meat we had apart from the lunch salami), and various dehydrated products. The most famous of these was TVP—Textured Vegetable Protein. It came in two flavours, bacon or mince, though no one was certain of the difference, and it was like chewing softened grit. It was nutritious and made you fart, or at least we pretended it did, because the stuff was so laughingly awful we had to make jokes about it. I had the food for one whole Christmas tramp organised around TVP, and, I have to admit, it did the trick.

Food was double-bagged and packed into aluminium tins, soldered up and posted down to an operator, who would fly in the tins to a bush airstrip. Usually you sent a map with the precise location pin-pointed, and rang the pilot to make sure the drop had gone in. These arrangements took time, so it was necessary to get the food down to the pilot at least a month before you left, which meant that it all had to be bought, sorted and packed before then. Usually we made a night of it, and some of the Christmas sherry never quite made it to its rightful destination.

It became an even more long-winded business, because you had to have your trip members sorted out before you could organise the food, so you could get the money off them, which then pushed the planning well back into spring. The food drop wasn't the only hassle. Flying was expensive, so if you were taking the train and ferry down, or the over-nighter on the *Rangatira* to Christchurch, bookings had to be made a good four to five months in advance to be sure of a place in the lemming-like Christmas rush south.

I suspect part of the reason that the Christmas tramping trip tradition existed in the first place was the rigid holiday schedule imposed by employers. You got a total of three weeks holiday a year, and for two weeks at Christmas the factories, the government offices, even many shops, were firmly closed.

So we lived and breathed Christmas trips—they were the highlight of the year and our entire yearly calendar was organised around them. First planning started in July, with a party assembled by July or August. Money was pooled by September and a deposit put down on the ferry and train transport. The food was organised (and the Tararua biscuits baked) by October, and sent down in November to be put in by chopper during December. Then finally the tramp itself took place over Christmas and New Year. You got your slides back by the end of January, and you might have a Christmas reunion and slide-showing in February, and some poor muggins would be conned into doing a write up for the journal. By March you were already scheming for the next Christmas tramp.

Oh yes, and there couldn't be bad weather. It wasn't allowed for in the organisation!

My first Christmas trip, led by Alan Parish, was to the Red Hills over the Christmas period of 1975–76. I'd just missed out on the previous Christmas, being rather a newcomer, and so had had to endure a whole year of boastful Christmas stories. Looking back on it, this trip was good as a first choice. We started by going up the Arawhata River for two days, then went up onto Mt Raddle and dropped down to the Cascade River, before climbing onto the Red Hill Range to the head of the Pyke River. We finished by coming back over Simonin Pass, down the Cascade to Martyr Saddle, and along Jackson Road to the Arawhata River again. A gigantic figure of eight in the Olivine Mountains.

The trip ran at a most leisurely pace, with two air-drops and five rest days. I think today I could do the whole trip in less than a week, but then we took eighteen days. There were ten of us, nine men and one woman, and we endured one horrendous day of rain and three days of cloud, but the rest were pure sunshine, so we all had blistered wee bodies when we came back.

Just getting down to the start at the Arawhata River was quite an epic. Three of us caught the *Rangatira* ferry overnight to Christchurch. This particular ferry took no cars and so there were miles of shiny,

Descent off Mt Raddle on a hot day, looking down on the Cascade River. On early maps this peak was called 'Mt Riddle', perhaps because of its strange bare red rocks. From right to left: Mike Hollis, Warren Thorburn, Alan Parish (leader), Grant Wheaton.

echoing passageways with small bunkrooms. At an hour when even God was still asleep (around five o'clock), the stewards banged on the doors, and shoved a half-cold, thoroughly stewed cup of tea in your face. We berthed at seven, caught the Lyttelton train to Christchurch, and then the Arthur's Pass train on Christmas Day to Greymouth, where we stayed at the motorcamp. On Boxing Day we picked up a hired minibus and driver, collected the others (who had rather sensibly taken the swifter means of getting south) at Hokitika airport and drove down to the Arawhata road bridge at Jackson Bay.

We pulled on our boots, getting them wet in the first minute by wading across the Jackson River, and camped on the riverbank at about six in the evening. I was in South Westland at last, after two days and two nights of travel.

What do I remember? Lots of things. Whether they are anything like the truth is debatable, but I do remember them. The vastness of the Arawhata Valley, for which I was psychologically unprepared. I knew the mountains were big, but not this big, and the width of the valley left me gasping—where was the river? The river flats were savannah lands of long grass, and we trailed through leaving swathes of crushed stalks behind us. I remember the unbearable heat as we slogged over the bare top of Mt Raddle, the long struggling climb up from the Cascade River onto the strange Red Hills themselves, and the terrible arguments that developed when we couldn't find water for lunch.

Some insisted that they *had* to stop for lunch, water or no water. Others equally insisted that without water, lunch was practically impossible. There was thick mist, we'd just broken out of the bush and everyone was tired. The leader made the decision to stop and as we grouchily gnawed our unsoftened Tararua biscuits, a waft of wind blew the mist away, and there before our marvelling eyes was a splendid tarn. As we rushed down to it, one member declared that it was already too late as he had already eaten *his* Tararua biscuits

I also remember the strange red rock, like sandpaper, on Simonin Pass, with the white stringy flecks of asbestos and the huge piled cairns which someone said had been built by Arawhata Bill. There was a long grotty day walking down the Cascade in rain—endless sidling and descending, then painful climbing again. At the end of the day we were buggered, had seen nothing, and risked our lives to cross a side-creek (see the Fools Creek story). I recall the intolerable mosquitoes in the Jackson valley. They were so bad that people got up in the middle of the night and lit a fire, and enjoyed, they assured us, ten excellent minutes from the moment the mozzies fell away, to the first chink of daylight when the sandflies started to bite.

We were off like rockets that morning, Hokitika and food beckoning. We met other tramping parties returning on the *Rangatira*, gossiped and boasted like crazy, and at 5.00 a.m. had another cup of cold tea, and a brilliant hot shower, like being incised with surgical needles. The showers on the *Rangatira* were justly famous, but that didn't stop them getting rid of the service. Many years later, in 1991, I was surprised to see the old *Rangatira* parked in the Helford River, in Cornwall, still in camouflage paint after being used as a troopship in the Falklands war.

All in all my first Christmas in the hills was memorable, which is not an unsalient point. A bad, wet Christmas tramp, where you get stuck in a hut for days, or worse, in a tent that has to have drains dug with your ice-axes, is no fun and can destroy a good keen tramper's appetite for tramping. I've seen it happen. This is the only two weeks holiday you have a year; you've been dreaming of it for six months and it starts to rain on the first evening. It rains and rains, then the rivers come up. You haven't moved. After six days you've had it and you bash out in a fury of frustration, temper and futility. It takes quite a lot of character to get back into the hills again after such a failure.

On one particularly grotty Christmas trip a fellow said he was so fed up he was going to get married when he got out. This was a surprise to his mates since he hadn't even mentioned that he had an 'intended'. In fact he didn't, but six months after the tramp he had met a girl, bedded her, engaged her and married her. No more bloody Christmas trips for him.

The next Christmas I went up the Otoko River to Marks Flat and the Landsborough valley, and the year after that it was Kahurangi National Park, which I organised and led. Then it was back into Aspiring country for two weeks to the head of the Arawhata and Trinity Col. During this time I'd joined a select club of trampers who could roll off a few names of remote places as casually as an order for fish and chips. In my own eyes I had gained a place for myself, some mana, some pride.

The fact that 99.9% of the population couldn't give a damn where I'd been, why I'd been there and what I'd suffered in getting there, was beside the point. I was only interested in the 0.1% of people who cared about these things.

Fools Creek

About halfway up the lower Cascade River in South Westland is a small side creek called Falls Creek. Small is a relative term, for it would match many full-sized North Island rivers, but by South Westland standards it was just a good-sized tiddler. About a week earlier we had crossed Mt Raddle from the Arawhata Valley and camped on the true right bank of Falls Creek, locating our food drop and discovering an old orange New Zealand Railways tarpaulin. After a leisurely day we continued up onto the Red Hills, leaving an impressive pile of firewood behind, as well as extra food, secure under the tarpaulin. Falls Creek was the linchpin of our trip, which was a circumnavigation of the Red Hills in a great figure of eight, and we expected to be back at this camp in about a week, all going well.

Everything did go well, apart from the day heading down the Cascade River. It had started to rain the night before, and as we bush-bashed down the top part of the Cascade River it set in heavily. We never saw Durward Falls, for we were endlessly sidling down in dense sodden bush. The rain was ceaseless, and we could hear the river roaring before we got to the banks of Falls Creek by about five o'clock in the afternoon. To me it looked massive. A great grey torrent of water gnawed down the riverbed, carrying black logs and boulders, clacking as it went. Two hundred metres away the creek was swallowed into the even vaster roaring torrent of the Cascade River. Anyone who crossed Falls Creek could not afford a mistake, for they would have no chance to right themselves before they were swept into the Cascade and that, as they say, would be that.

I was new to tramping, and this was my first big trip and my first serious river crossing. The group decided we should cross, so that's what we did. There must have been some debate about the matter, but the clincher was the comfortable camp site, stash of food and pile of dry firewood that lay under the tarpaulin only 100 metres away. We were soaked, tired and miserable, and the prospect of eking out a wet night with wet gear was unappealing.

Hindsight reveals it stopping raining by seven that evening, and the next morning the creek had dropped by half its height. But we were not prophets, rather, we suspected the creek could come up more and trap us for days. Grant Wheaton got out his axe and chopped two big poles, one each for five people.

The leader divvied out the positions, putting the most experienced and weightiest at the top, and the lightest in the middle. The concept was simple. The pole was threaded through our arms and held close to the chest, then everyone locked arms together making a secure unit. The group advanced slowly into the creek at right angles to the current, with the top man taking the force of the river, whilst the others, being relatively protected from the current in slacker water, supported him.

Someone experienced usually took the down-river end of the pole, for it was crucial that the line of trampers stayed parallel to the current. If they got twisted off centre then the pressure would fall on all the weaker members as well, and if they got knocked off their feet then it was all over. At all costs people had to hang onto the pole even if they got swept off their feet. Which was probably easier said than done, and none of us particularly wanted to put it to the test.

Above the roar of the river I was told to go on the first crossing and positioned at number two, with Warren Thorburn taking the top of the pole. He had size and experience, and he needed it. Below me I think was Shirley Morrison and Hugh Middleton, and at the bottom was Paul Aubrey. We had what looked like a hundred metres of angry water to get across, but it was in all probability only 20 metres or so. There was not much hesitation and I don't remember being at all scared—at first.

Almost immediately we were up to our knees in the current, and then our hips. Warren was doing well and we were edging slowly towards the far bank. The boulders were moving rapidly underneath, making it

Crossing the Williamson River in 1979, using the arms over shoulder link-up method.

difficult to get purchase. It was hard to tell from the bank where the main force of the current was, but once we were in the water it became obvious: it was on the far side. This was not encouraging.

If the deepest part had been close to our side of the creek then we could have tested it with more margin of safety and had a chance of retreat. If you must retreat then you have to shuffle *backwards* out of the river; at first this sounds daft, but there really is no other way. With a pole linking you it's impossible to swing around in mid-current. We would have been swept off our feet, and even if we had managed to hang together at all costs, we would have floated down towards the Cascade River quite out of control. With the deepest part of the creek on the far side there was really no likelihood of being able to retreat back-

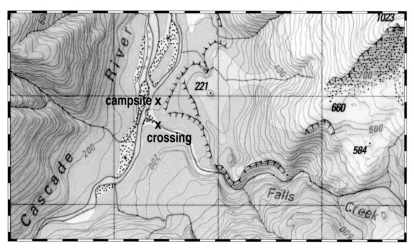

Falls Creek and campsite.

wards across the whole of Falls Creek. We were utterly committed.

Near the strongest part of the creek Warren was starting to sweat. He was up to his waist and leaning so far over into the roaring river that his legs were getting tangled in mine, and several times we were in dire danger of tripping ourselves up. I was on a tremendous lean as well, and focusing mainly on trying to keep my legs out of his way. Warren's face was contorted with the exertion needed to fight against the current. Boulders were bashing into our legs, and most of the time I was struggling to get more than one good foot purchase at a time. Warren was yelling instructions, but I doubt if anyone could hear a thing. The noise was tremendous, and at the deepest part of the creek the velocity was enormous, with the backwash up to my chest.

We were inching closer, but it seemed to take forever. Probably the whole crossing only took a minute and a half, and we were only in the worst part for less than 20 seconds. Just another foot, maybe another, we could see calm water, just a foot more...

Done it! We collectively threw ourselves into the calm water, which was still waist deep, but the pressure was behind us, and we disengaged from the pole and scrabbled up onto good solid earth. The gasps of relief are still vivid in my mind. We slapped each other and joked about it being 'borderline', and stupidly turned and watched the other crew make their move, and perhaps it was at that moment that I felt the most queasy. I could see the tall figure of Mike Hollis at the top of the pole, barely poking out of some of the troughs and crests of the brown current. They were struggling as we had, and it was gruesome watching them creep into the deepest part of the current facing the same final test we had. But they had one crucial advantage. They knew that if we'd done it, they could do it too.

We raced to the campsite and threw up the tents while the dry firewood was ignited in a great and glorious burst of relief. I can't remember what was said that evening, probably some gung-ho stuff, but I do remember that late that night, as the rain cleared away from the skies, I lay in my sleeping bag and kept going over the river crossing in my mind. Over and over. Perhaps the crossing was not as deep or as swift as I imagined it, but it made a lasting impression. It was my first major flooded river, and I felt brave, proud and slightly foolish, for I felt then what I still feel today. There was no need to have risked our lives for a bundle of dry firewood.

Tussock grasses in Toaroha River, West Coast.

CHAPTER TWO

HIGH COUNTRY

This short chapter celebrates what Samuel Butler called 'the extreme back-country', which we now call the high country. From his hut doorstep in 1860 Butler could see higher mountains still, bracketed with plateaus of ice, and this formidable country became 'Erewhon' in his novel of the same name, a land where range after range had to be penetrated and overcome before the final shangri-la could be reached.

Butler's satire is scarcely ever read now, wisely I think, since the joke about musical banks (i.e. churches) seems unconscionably Victorian in its tone. But the high country remains, with its broad tussock downlands that seem at first static, almost devoid of life, but paradoxically are brimful of movement—a lone falcon sweeping over the hills; the curl of cloud on a mountain top; the bolt of a hare through the tussock.

This enduring, edgy landscape never got under Butler's pommy skin; he doubled his money in four years, then shook the Rangitata River dust off his boots and never returned. But I keep returning, and the mystery of the high country for me is that there is so much to see in such an empty land.

No Exit to Erewhon

How absurd, from a philosophical point of view, that the shingle roads leading into the mountains are marked No Exit: nothing could be further from the truth. They are not so much road ends as a means to an end, the starting point for adventure and mystery; and one of the great unintentional fringe benefits of being a keen tramper is that you end up a de facto explorer of some of the best and most secret back-country roads in New Zealand.

These are the roads that twist and twine through high-country foothills and valleys, grinding over dusty saddles named after 'Jack' and descending to the final ford, where inevitably travellers to the mountainous holy land will get a baptism whether they like it or not. There is the dark road that slithers into the King Country of the Matemateaongas and gets swallowed by papa tunnels before worming its way to the sudden squelchy stop of a cow paddock. There are sunlit roads that turn behind the Canterbury foothills to reveal a magical opening between two ranges; and roads that leave a long dust plume behind them as the travellers eventually, and nervously, arrive on the homestead doorstep.

Over the 1970s and '80s we had a touching faith that our Hillman Hunters, Cortinas, Morris Oxfords and Austin Maxis would deliver us to these remote road ends, and by and large our faith was justified. If they got stuck we could push; if they broke down we could scratch our heads, and by and by we'd get them started again.

Few people had four-wheel-drive vehicles in the 1980s, and Hillman Hunters, though not easily stopped by hills, were quickly defeated by a wet patch. For example, just 200 metres beyond Glen Lyon Station in the Dobson River valley was a large boggy mire on the road, which the farmer did not seem in a particular hurry to drain. No doubt he had his reasons. So my friend and I abandoned the car and slogged along for 25 kilometres on the hard shingle track to the first station hut, arriving after dark—and not before walking into a stroppy cow.

We were having a well-deserved sleep-in in the morning when a rumble announced the farmer turning up in his Land Rover.

'I wondered where you boys got to last night,' he said. 'Yer didn't walk all that way, did yer? I could have given yer a lift. Must be keen buggers.'

At the end of most high-country roads is the farmer. Despite the fact that all the back-country land was supposedly sold long ago to Americans, the same larger-than-life, laconic, sometimes garrulous, big-hearted Kiwi farmer and his team of excitable dogs is still there. Only two or three times can I recall being unreasonably refused access by a farmer; 99% of the time permission was freely given, usually with a few topographical hints:

'Just follow the track past the shed, then take a header up the hill, swing through the paddock past the bulls (generally quiet this time of year), cross over the electric fence (don't think it's switched on, but don't rely on me) and when yer see the deer fence take a bearing left and yer can't miss it.'

You are normally well on your way through his land before you realise you've forgotten to ask what it is you 'can't miss'.

I well remember coming out of the Richmond Range at the end of a hot Easter tramp in 1975, and being met at Mt Patriarch Station by an extraordinary gentlemen resembling Long John Silver, peg leg and all. I subsequently found out that his name was Whacka Anderson. He and his menagerie of tame dogs, cats and goats welcomed us, and he threw great slabs of bread and butter at the tired trampers who gobbled it all down with thick sweet tea. The 1906 cob farmhouse was chock-full of rotting pig heads and rusting farm implements, but what impressed me most was Whacka's bellowing voice that echoed up to the macrocarpa trees calling 'Cockie! Cockie!', whereupon two tame cockatoos (which he said had cost him $200 apiece from Aussie) came screaming down and landed heavily on either shoulder to start fossicking in his ears.

When you ring up a farmer a few days beforehand he will most likely want to size you up first, and will say, 'Look into the station on the way, will yer,' forcing you to present yourself for a good grilling on your tactics, aspirations and general manner of living. Some remotely situated farmers work up a real head of steam, and the unfortunate visitor gets a thrashing over the hot political potato of the day and is made to feel that in some obscure way asking for permission to cross the farmer's land is directly related to unemployed bludgers, Labour lefties rotting the body politic, or townie greenies who wouldn't know the front from the arse-end of a sheep. Probably they're right; at least we nod politely and know that the spleen will be vented in time.

One high-country farmer, Lawrie Prouting of Mesopotamia Station, was famous for his harangues to trampers, including the observation, 'If you can't climb Mt Cook you shouldn't be bloody walking over my land.' On one particular occasion, after 30 minutes of such sentiments, my mate started arguing back. Oh God! They went at it hammer and tongs, and I was sure blood was going to be spilt on the fine high-country tussock, until suddenly, after an hour and a half of fierce debate, Lawrie hopped back on his tractor and said, 'Cheery. Good talking to you boys, have a great trip.' We did.

'Stations' were so called because the farmer 'stationed' himself in the best position for managing and claiming his run. Many early high-country stations were established before any legal survey, so boundaries were often set by vague notions such as 'up to the Snowy Mountains'. It was quite common for sheep station boundaries to include all notable local peaks; Butler's old station at Mesopotamia, for instance, went as high as Mt D'Archiac at 2876 metres.

But times change and nowadays the unproductive higher slopes are being retired in return for freeholding the better pasture on the valley floor. Some merinos are managed intensively at low altitudes for fine wool, deer farms have been established and fenced hunting blocks attract 'big game' hunters. So the image of the high-country station lifestyle is especially evocative now because we are witnessing the moment of its passing.

Sidling above Potts River with Mt D'Archiac behind, creating its own cloud plume.

Gone is the canny shepherd garbed in his long brown musterer's coat, working his hack up the scree slopes and squinting into the sunset at the last stubborn ewe to be brought down to the mob. These days the musterer might spot the mobs with a helicopter, use a farm bike to get up the track and a cellphone to keep in touch with the gang. That's what they do on Mt Buster, I saw it on the telly.

In Pursuit of
Sergeant Garvey

Some tramping trips start from little more than a dot on the map, and one of those dots had always intrigued me—Sergeant Garvey's cairn.

This was a man who had fought at Balaclava in the Crimean War at the age of 20, and participated in the famous charge of the Light Brigade on 26 September 1854. How had he survived that, yet come to die nine years later in September 1863 in a blizzard in Central Otago?

The sergeant's cairn is found in the Buster Basin near Naseby, a pure high-country area of tussock and rock savannah with not a smudge of bush, and pestered with four-wheel-drive tracks. I could imagine a route that went over Mt Buster, threading through old gold sluicings down to the cairn, and then returning over the tops. I reasoned that summer would be too hot for tramping there though, so I settled on late August—pleasant spring weather with just a skiff of snow.

Sven Brabyn and I arrived on the tail end of a southerly buster, with mist and cold flakes of snow filtering the sun, which made the ruined sluices look like pillars of gold salt. It had taken two hours up the deep snow-filled track to reach the lip of the plateau at 1200 metres, and I was wearing full storm gear and my double-thick balaclava. The 'hut' on the map turned out to be an empty shed and the temperature was a tropical minus seven that night. Outside the wind-chill made it minus twelve. Pleasant spring weather.

Mt Buster was originally called 'Mt Burster' and the diggings (also sometimes called 'Clarkes') were opened in August 1863, but proved a disappointment to most. Bremmer Bros store opened at the foot of the hill, but other diggings flared up at Hamiltons and Kyeburn and everyone rushed there without giving Mt Burster a second thought, except for a few determined parties. Their names are dotted on the side-gullies and hills in the Buster basin, and in one wash Messrs Grogarty and Greer were reputed to have retrieved over 1000 ounces (28 kilograms) of gold!

Historic sluicings at the Mt Buster diggings.

The next morning Sven and I tramped down through the white-out to Guffies Creek, and were amazed to see pipits bobbing cheerily in and out of the frozen snow-tussock. We were retracing part of the route taken by poor Sergeant Garvey of the Otago Armed Constabulary, the main difference being that he was utterly lost.

In September 1863 he and a companion were dispatched by his superior, Sergeant Ryan, to check out the new diggings on Mt Burster. On their return from the Burster diggings a storm overtook them on the plateau, and they sheltered behind a large rock at the head of the Little

Kye Burn. Sergeant Garvey was determined to continue, but his companion, Constable MacDonald, wanted to wait because, as he shouted to Garvey when the Sergeant rode off into the storm, 'You're going the wrong way.'

In thick fog these Otago peneplains are hopelessly featureless, but by the time we reached the Guffies Creek outstation the mist had burnt off and the skies were a stunning blue. We dropped our packs and headed over the hill into Hut Creek to find out where Sergeant Garvey had ended up. It is a romantic place for death. Great rock outcrops loom over the memorial cairn, and a new bronze plaque has been installed (presumably) by the Police Association, which reads:

> *Edward John Garvey, sergeant Otago Armed Constabulary Force. Died 24th September 1863 in a snowstorm, while on duty, aged 29 years.*

It is surprising how far Sergeant Garvey managed to come from the top diggings. After he left the shelter rock he must have obliviously turned 180 degrees and, instead of descending into the Little Kye Burn, blundered back down past the new Burster sluicings and the diggers in their storm-bound huts, and some ten kilometres into the Otematata River headwaters. It's not hard to imagine him blinded by snow, urging on his tired horse, confused by the landscape and befuddled with cold. The memorial cairn is built beside some large rock outcrops, some of which might have offered shelter to him, and there is also dried matagouri on the river flats that would have made a fire, but by now the sergeant was presumably too far gone to help himself.

Meanwhile Constable MacDonald managed to get out to Naseby with frostbitten feet and sound the alarm. The relief party was led by William Morrison, and they set off four days later, with not much hope of finding the sergeant alive. The blizzard had turned into rain and washed away much of the snow, and they eventually found Sergeant Garvey 'lying peacefully on his back'. He was lashed onto a pack horse and taken to Dunedin.

The next day we tramped up Long Spur under circling New Zealand falcons, and several plump Himalayan chukar exploded out of the tussocks and whirred into the brilliant sky. Two paradise ducks flew overhead and skylarks started to sing as the sun warmed the air. To the west were huge bare plateaus of grassland, impressionistic with snow, and we could see the lone dot of a hut several kilometres away.

That evening the nor'wester howled over the bleak peneplain and we happily dived down for shelter to the musterers' top hut, which sits at an altitude of 1371 metres. 'Blue Duck Hut: the packers nightmare' is etched on the door.

What a place to spend your working life: not a tree, not a skerrick of a shrub. All fuel would have to be packed in up to the boundary keeper, and perhaps that's what made it a 'nightmare'. There were no signatures on the anorexic tin walls, but there was wood and rotten sacks of coal piled in a neglected corner, and it was strangely comforting to be enjoying a snug fire at an altitude where the nearest trees were at least 900 metres lower.

Men like their stories, and in solitary iron huts the kernel of a fire is nursed in the same manner that a story is elaborated; pieces of fuel added to keep the flame going, but not so fast so as to burn yourself out of story-telling material. The old shepherds must have talked about Sergeant Garvey as we did. Sven reckoned he died a useless death, and it's hard to avoid that conclusion.

He made so many mistakes: leaving the rock shelter, ignoring the advice of his companion, overconfident in his sense of direction. His horse survived and was found beside the sergeant's frozen body, eating snowgrass. But heroes are always in short supply, and Sergeant Garvey must do. This was one of the 600 men who had charged poetically into 'the valley of death', as Alfred Lord Tennyson intoned, which, when you come to think about it, was another lot of useless deaths.

We got back to the carpark well satisfied with our little high-country circuit, which we walked entirely on four-wheel-drive tracks. We had joined dots together, crossed creeks named after the men who built the water races, and followed Sergeant Garvey to his doom. His over-sub-scribed funeral fund helped build Naseby hospital, and the sergeant got a hero's burial, a fine stone monument in Dunedin, and his name etched on topographical maps for all eternity. But what was so noble about his 'duty', which consisted of deserting his companion and making a selfish run for it down to the warm fires in the Hogburn a few hundred metres below?

History has treated Sergeant Garvey rather generously, which just goes to show that very little grows on the harsh high-country plateaus of Central Otago except tussock and a good story.

The Swaggers

Swaggers were once part and parcel of the high country, as indeed they were part of the infrastructure of a young colony. For almost a hundred years of New Zealand's pioneer history, from 1850 to the 1930s, there was a whole army of casual labourers, foot-slogging to sheep stations for seasonal shearing, or wheat farms for reaping and binding work, or carrying their pan and shovel to the goldfields. In a young colonial land you had to work hard and walk long distances—people did not need to get fit in nineteenth-century New Zealand, they already were.

They [swaggers] walked to walk. If there was no work and no dole, time on the road did not much matter. A fortnight would take a man across most of the South Island. They erected calico tents in the trees near the fresh water and were ready to start when the season and the boss willed. They erected 'tents' of pine boughs in many an Otago or Canterbury plantation, and the concertinas might come out around the fire and voices might sing Alice Ben Bolt *or* The Wild Colonial Boy.

Labour was cheap and could be moved on. It was a time when men were proud of their physical achievements in a poorly mechanised society, and they were swaggers in all senses of the word. John A. Lee recalls his swagging days:

> *While fifteen years of age [about 1917] I had tramped from Burnham to Temuka, from Burnham to Rangitata, from Burnham to Glenavy. Before I was eighteen I had walked from Dunedin to Roxburgh, back to Lawrence, when three hundred goldwinners and their families could attend a Scots concert at nowadays deserted Blue Spur at the top of Gabriel's Gully.*
>
> *I walked from Tuapeka to Invercargill, from Invercargill to Lumsden, from Invercargill to Christchurch. Long before I was twenty I had walked from Masterton through the Manawatu Gorge to Wanganui, thence by the Feilds Track, papa in those days, to the Main Trunk, from Auckland to Ohakune, from Auckland to Feilding, from Auckland to Otamatea, and so on.*
>
> *On many a Hallowe'en, my birthday, I slept in the tussocks or under the gorse hedges, or burrowed into a straw stack, or in a shed or a stable, in the fern in Auckland province on a summer night... I have lived on handouts, sit down feeds, and once for days on boiled mangel and rocksalt.*
>
> —Shining with the Shiner

John A. Lee experienced the swagging life as a teenager, and 20 years later he was a brand new member of the cabinet that passed the Social Security Bill of 1938, which gave a pension to everyone over 65—and made swagging a choice, not a necessity.

The high country, and the generous station owners, attracted the last of the swaggers, and even into the 1940s there were still a few old-timers choosing this life. 'John the Baptist' was a well-known swagger who for years tramped around the back-country stations of Canterbury, doing his 'round of inspection' up one side of the Rakaia River to Glenfalloch, then across to Manuka Point and Algidus stations, down the other side to Glentunnel and back to Christchurch. He was once offered a lift but declined, saying in complete seriousness, 'Goodness me, that would never do. I would miss all my customers on my round of inspection.' When asked how he crossed the big rivers like the Rakaia and the Wilberforce he gave the famous reply, 'The Lord helped me.'

Mona Anderson mentions John the Baptist in her book *The Good Logs of Algidus.* When he turned up unexpectedly at her Greymouth home, after hitching and sleeping in a railway wagon, he played her a jig on his mouth organ. Perhaps the continuing appeal of people like Arawhata Bill, who after all achieved nothing in his life except immortality, is that the idea of packing a swag and escaping to the hills is still a seductive one. In that sense, modern-day tramping still has an element of old-fashioned swagging in it.

The only swagger I ever met (apart from a fellow carrying a sugar sack and walking with bare feet on the main Kaimai range) was up the Lawrence River, one of the three branches of the Rangitata River, in the early 1980s. He was heading down to Erewhon Station at Jumped-Up Downs on a stinking hot day, trudging along in corduroy trousers with an old wooden-framed Trapper Nelson pack and some sort of dusty felt hat on his head. He was about 40, I suppose, scruffy and bearded and probably on the dole. I didn't catch his name, but he was personable and chatty, and explained that he was doing an Arthur's Pass to Mt Cook traverse—though it was a most peculiar one.

He was not going over the alpine passes at all, but had wandered his way up and down the sides of the big shingle valleys like the Harper River and Avoca River, then on to the Wilberforce, Mathias and Rakaia, and was walking across Lake Heron Station to the Rangitata River when I met him. So far he had taken three months just to do that bit.

What puzzled me was how he managed the river crossings. Most of these braided rivers can be crossed fairly easily at the right time of the year, particularly at Easter, but if he could not make it then he just stayed on the same bank until he found a bridge! The first road bridge across the Wilberforce River is right down by State Highway 72, and so he walked 50 kilometres all the way to it, then repeated the performance 50 kilometres back into the Rakaia valley. It had taken him a week, so he said, just for that section.

As far as I could work out he was 'living off the land', which meant eating hut food. In the early 1980s the New Zealand Forest Service still stashed food in their huts and it was not at all unusual to come across cupboards full of tinned lamb tongues, tinned peaches and cartons of tasty Weetbix, long since metamorphosed into cardboard. Still, good tucker for a solo swagger. There were station huts as well, so this fellow raided a hut, lived in it till he had exhausted the supplies (or the cockie discovered him and kicked him out) and moved onto the next—like a travelling vacuum cleaner with boots.

He immediately reminded me of swaggers like John the Baptist and seemed content, though I think he would have disliked being called a hermit. He was just doing his own thing and had chosen the backblocks to do it, but I wished I'd asked him a question I have often put to myself: is the back country an escape or a refuge?

The Mouse

The sun was fast shrinking from the tops as I came over from the Lowburn pack track in the Pisa Range and looked down on Meg Hut. There was fresh snow on the ground, and I barely had time to get to the hut, chop some wood and get a fire roaring in the cavernous fireplace before the sun switched off and autumn dark wrapped itself around the old musterers' hut. It was made of thin corrugated iron with no lining, and had eight sacking bunks and a big old table against one wall under the small window. The wall ornaments consisted of metal objects belonging to the fading musterers' art: a bridle bit, a horseshoe and an empty whisky bottle. After a second cup of tea I huddled by the fire and became aware that I was sharing the hut that night.

Little whiskers poked out, attracted by the fire and the prospect of a feed. Tiny feet pattered along the darkened table and there was a glint of eyes from behind the billy. I watched for some time and considered my approach. It was a bitterly cold night, lonely and stark, and to some extent I welcomed the company. Of course any conversation would be somewhat one way, but better than talking to the empty whisky bottle. It seemed rather churlish to attempt to exterminate the little mouse when his only crime was hunger.

I poked about in my pack and found a crumbled mass of bread that had once formed a loaf and, taking a handful, rolled it into a ball, placed it on the table beside the billy and waited for a response. The whiskers had disappeared with my movements, but not for long, so the mouse was either brave or hungry. It rapidly retraced its steps back to the billy, sniffed around suspiciously and then dashed behind the bread ball and peered out. It clearly had not yet realised that the fist-sized object it was lurking behind was composed entirely of food—a veritable mountain of delight, four times larger than itself. It sniffed curiously. There was food around here somewhere, it was sure.

Great Mice in Heaven! The mouse reared up on its back legs, eyes wide open in astonishment. I can still see the look of utter amazement and panic on its face. What to do? In a second it had pushed, pummelled and propelled the globe of bread off the table, and leapt in a suicidal fashion after it. As the bread rolled under the table the mouse was tussling with it from behind and, with all its might, rolled the bread ball into a dark corner by a hole. With a final heave the bread and mouse were through the hole and gone.

I had lost my furry companion, and rather regretfully, had to go back to talking to the empty whisky bottle.

Fireplace Fred is his name
This resident mouse is quite tame
If you leave out a biscuit
He'll come out and risk it
While leaving your pack as it came

Trust Poulter Hut, Arthur's Pass, 21 February 1987, anonymous.

Red markers on tree stump, Bealey Spur, Arthur's Pass.

CHAPTER THREE

MAKING TRACKS

I t is puzzling that we put such a high value on historic buildings yet do not consider the roads and tracks that lead to them. Indeed you could argue that the first historic sites in New Zealand were camp-fires and tracks. Many routes in the back country are over 100 years old, and some, like Harper Pass, can claim an 800-year history.

The tracks used by Maori were subtle and discreet; the snap of a twig, the imprint of a foot on moss—the last thing you wanted was for the track to reveal your presence to your enemies. Trails went where food and shelter could be found. European tracks, on the other hand, were made with different cultural assumptions: living off the land was less important than speed through it, and they bustled through the mountains, heading bluntly to a remote bush logging settlement or a newly discovered goldfield.

It's possible on old tracks to detect a century of track marking. A 'tree blaze' cut by a slasher might have a piece of New Zealand Forest Service white permolat (venetian blind material) nailed into it, while on a neighbouring tree there is a new Department of Conservation bright orange triangle. Occasionally you find yourself following a discreet culler's track up a long bushy spur to the tops, marked here and there with the rusty lids of tin cans nailed to trees. On old maps the word 'disced' is scribed beside the track.

This chapter follows an historic pathway of its own and goes one step beyond into bush bashing, where the only track is the one we make ourselves.

Harper Pass:
An 800-year-old Track

The first time I crossed Harper Pass it was a wet dismal day. The scrub was overladen with snow, and the wind cut through my old japara parka as if I were wearing a summer shirt. I got down to the first hut on the Hurunui side of the pass and was disappointed to find a small 'dog kennel' biv, that even the dogs would have sniffed their noses at. So I thrashed on down through the headwaters of the Hurunui River, getting muddied by the creeks, and reached No. 3 Hut, cold and saturated, my fingers so sodden with the rain they were like prunes on sticks. The hut was cavernous and empty, and I built up the fire in the woodbox and made various New Year resolutions to buy better gear—but who would have expected snow at Christmas?

Since then I have been over the pass several times, on sunny days and grey days. I've seen the Taramakau River in a lathering torrent and the Hurunui River so dry you could hardly find a decent-sized pool to jump in. I've bathed luxuriously in the Hurunui hot pool, surrounded by wispy falling snow, and I've slept in every hut along the way, including three that are no longer there.

All the time on these crossings I've wondered about the history of the Harper Pass track, for here was a trail that could boast perhaps 800 years of travellers. From the first Waitaha explorers who pushed into the unknown and Ngai Tahu greenstone parties, to hurrying gold-diggers and drovers driving their unhappy flocks of sheep through the alpine scrublands—this is one of the most historic tracks in New Zealand. It has a chequered history, going through periods of intense use then lapsing into obscurity again, yet it's never been totally forgotten.

Harper Pass straddles the main divide of the Southern Alps at the low altitude of 962 metres. The two approach rivers—the Taramakau and Hurunui—follow a conveniently straight fault-line, and on one early map the pass is marked as 'Saddle Taramakau, Te Rau o Tama'. Hurunui possibly means 'flowing hair', and according to the Waitaha people the Taramakau River was named 'Tatara Makau'. One derivation of Taramakau means 'flowing bend in the river'. Europeans got into a tongue-twisting pother with the name and called it anything from 'terrible cow' to 'tether my cow' to 'Terry McCow'.

What brought Maori to Harper Pass in the first place? One suggestion is that they were following the paths of moa. There were several species of moa, including three sub-alpine ones, and they must have left trails through the easy tussock and beech country of the Hurunui, crossing low passes like Harper Pass to the West Coast. Maori explorers would have forged a route that followed the moa on summer forays, scouting, hunting, camping and feasting as they went, then retreating in winter. Later they explored all the way to the West Coast, linking up with Maori down the coastline, and between them found the greenstone country that turned the pass into a strategic highway.

It has been estimated that a large Maori family group might have taken 15 to 20 days to cover the 350 kilometres from the West Coast, via Lake Brunner and Harper Pass, and around Lake Sumner to Kaiapoi pa. At a speed of around three kilometres an hour they would be able to travel 15 to 20 kilometres in a five- or six-hour day, which is not so very different from a modern tramping party, although the Maori parties would have had to stop regularly to replace their paraerae (flax sandals—it took 20 minutes to make a pair that lasted two days), snare food and make shelters. War parties regularly made the trip in five to seven days.

Deep rivers were crossed by Maori either on rafts called mokihi, made out of bundled flax stalks, or by using the technique of a breast pole known as tuwhana. Maori packs, or kawe, show an uncanny similarity to modern packs.

Once, in a flat area of rainforest in the Taramakau Valley I undertook the experiment of trying to make a trail as Maori did. I bent the undersides of silver fern so that the paler side was exposed, I broke branches off and let them dangle, I trod moss patches very firmly, I pulled off strips of bark, and then went in a large exploratory circle trying to pick up the trail I had made ten minutes earlier. I never could find it again.

Europeans quickly took advantage of the low pass, with Edward Dobson, in the company of local runholders G. E. Mason, Taylor and Dampier, reaching the pass in 1857. Leonard Harper, guided by Ihaia Tainui, crossed the pass that same year, at the age of 20, and both these young men subsequently became Members of Parliament.

In 1862, the possibility of gold on the West Coast encouraged the Canterbury Provincial Government to employ Charlton Howitt to cut a track over the pass. When the gold rush came in 1865 this primitive trail was rendered almost impassable by hundreds of feverish gold-diggers heading to the coast. They were followed by farmers driving mobs of cattle and sheep, and grog shanties and butcher stores sprang up along the route. But the track's popularity immediately waned when the much more direct Arthur's Pass track was cut in the winter of 1865.

In 1884 Arthur Dudley Dobson (of Arthur's Pass fame) was employed by the Public Works Department to survey a railway line over the Hurunui Saddle, and there was an extensive public debate over whether the railway should cross Harper Pass or Arthur's Pass. Dobson was impressed by the hot pools in the Hurunui River and wondered if they would make a health resort, but the road, the railway and public interest went elsewhere.

The old gold-diggers track remained, however, and it was by following this trail that George Park, with his brother James, made an astonishing trip in 1889. He canoed from Hokitika to Christchurch, via the Taramakau and Hurunui Rivers, manhandling the canoes across Harper Pass. These were home-built canoes made from strips of native timber (kauri and cedar was one combination) glued and screwed together and weighing about 45 kilograms each. The epic trip took thirteen days to cover the 368 kilometres, and it is doubtful it has ever been repeated—or is likely to be.

The Harper Pass route lapsed into obscurity until 1936–1939 when the Physical Welfare branch of the Department of Internal Affairs decided to establish a popular tramping track. It was during the Depression and great energy was being put into improving the public health of New Zealanders. The old gold-diggers route was re-opened and several large huts built and labelled with splendid bureaucratic imagination: No. 1, No. 2, and No. 3 on the Hurunui side, and Locke Stream on the Taramakau side. The intention was to guide large parties through, but the Second World War put paid to the scheme, and once again Harper Pass tracks became overgrown.

No. 2 Hut beside Lake Sumner, subsequently burnt down in 2000.

By the 1970s the New Zealand Forest Service had become 'user friend-ly' and they spruced up the old Physical Welfare huts, added a couple of their own (Hope–Kiwi and Halfway Shelter), re-cut the track and advertised it through pamphlets and brochures. It was a sort of early 'Great Walk', and with public bus transport to either end, it enjoyed a brief tramping boom, becoming the track 'you had to do'.

But by the late 1980s the Department of Conservation had devel-oped other Great Walks with high track standards and no river cross-ings, and the interest in Harper Pass waned, though it remains quietly popular amongst Canterbury trampers to this day.

Like the river, the track has changed, and yet in many ways remains the same. Very little in the geography of Harper Pass has changed in the past 800 years. Some birds have become extinct, some new birds have invaded. New mammalian predators now squat in the valleys, but the track and the modern tramper still follow the logical sinews of the land, crossing at the best fords, scrambling up around the short gorges and pausing on the vast river flats, just as Maori trampers must have paused and adjusted their kawe on straining shoulders hundreds of years before.

Pick and Shovel

Perhaps in another 800 years people will marvel over the long strips of tarseal that interlace our communities in the way that we now marvel over Stonehenge. What could have possessed them to build these 'mo-torways' and 'highways', they will ask? Their resources were so meagre, their skills so limited, yet their highways are found everywhere, leading without apparent purpose to obscure destinations and arbitrarily finishing at dead ends. Well, I feel the same way about pack tracks.

What strangely wonderful structures they are, wriggling into the back country through deep cuttings, with bluffs dynamited and banks supported by dry-walling, the careful gradient calculated with no more precise tool than a hand plumb-line and a practical eye. They are unsung masterpieces of engineering, so subtle that we race over them in complete disregard for the effort and pain that has bled into every yard.

Far more pack tracks exist than are shown on modern maps. They have disappeared into the bush and tussocks until only passing deer or sheep take advantage of them. We stumbled on one concealed in thick beech forest in Larry's Creek in the Victoria Range, probably built originally to access a mine shaft; and many years ago we stumbled across the 'Cascade to Hollyford Road' in dense South Westland bush (see The Red Hills story). The famous 'zig-zag' pack track at the foot of Browning Pass is still visible 140 years after it was built, and the route dynamited through the bluffs was still being used 15 years ago, though slips have now destroyed parts of it.

Pack tracks are proud, somewhat forlorn leftovers from an earlier period of industrialisation. At the time they were a signal of ambition and progress, and it is ironic that, rather like Stonehenge, we find them romantic. They serviced the infrastructure of the young colony, like the pack track over Browning Pass, or avoided awkward pieces of coastline on the West Coast, like the Paringa Cattle Track. Some, such as the Croesus Track in the Paparoas, went up to gold mines, and others were entirely conceived and built as tourist trails, such as the track to Welcome Flats in the Copland River and the track up to Alex Knob in Franz Josef.

These types of track were all designed to be wide and level enough for pack animals with side panniers. They were made with pick and shovel by men living in tents beside the road who were paid ten shillings a day. Often this sort of rough work went to unemployed gold-miners, and councils used the road schemes as a means of soaking up surplus labour that might otherwise prove troublesome. Contractual obligations were explicit. Usually the track had to be cleared to a specified width, anything from five to 30 feet, then formed or benched between four and nine feet, then metalled for the final four to five foot width. Even the depth of metalling was precise, which for many pack tracks was six inches.

History has mostly forgotten the road-makers, but there is something about these nineteenth-century pack tracks that suggests to me that the men who made them did their job proudly. If you look closely you can see hand-crafted stone culverts, where the slabs of rock have been split, laid and locked together so well that even after a century they still function perfectly. This wasn't just jobbing work but the work of skilled men—'working class athletes', John A. Lee called them—who were mostly anonymous, leading a hard life alleviated only by the surreptitious clink of a 'nobbler' from a whisky bottle, and a song and a yarn in a Celtic accent.

Bush Bashing

The expression 'bush' is popularly supposed to derive from Australian back-country jargon, and one early Australian source for the word dates from 1826: 'they go into the interior, or bush, as it is termed'. However, in the early nineteenth century the word 'bush' was used in almost every English speaking country, with examples from Canada, South Africa and even the United States. Its origin is obscure, though it may have originated from the Dutch word 'bosch', meaning sparsely settled or out of town.

From this blunt word sprang all manner of colourful expressions, particularly from Australia: 'going bush' (heading out into the back country for a while), 'getting bushed' (lost), 'bush fever' (being too long in the hills), 'bush telegraph' (rumour and gossip) and 'bushman' (someone who is skilled in bushcraft). There are also 'bush carpenter' (rough and ready) and 'bush lawyer' (without legal qualifications). Some expressions did not leap the ditch to New Zealand, including 'bushranger', 'bush pickles' (a bottle of worcester sauce mixed with plum jam) and the laconic 'bushman's breakfast' (a drink of water followed by a look around).

Then there is 'bush bashing', which seems to be an unlovely and peculiarly exact New Zealand word (the *Oxford English Dictionary* does not list it) to describe travel off the track. Bush bashing is the point where the track stops and you make your own way, just as the early Maori or adventurous gold-diggers did. It's a skill, except one would be hard pressed to define exactly where the skill lies.

One of the great satisfactions of tramping is to navigate a 'clean' way through difficult country and extract the essence of the route: to look at the lie of the land, to study the map, then choose a route that precisely and economically delivers you to the target destination. It's a curious pleasure to explain because it involves a subtle combination of skills: observation, planning, tactics, foresight and risk. If I can borrow another word for it, it is about flow, and everyone has a sense of it. A hunter experiences it when a hunt succeeds; likewise a general whose strategy works, or a mother bringing the complex elements of a pre-schooler's birthday party to a successful conclusion. It works or it doesn't, and when it does work, it flows.

In the Gunner Downs it did not flow. No one really goes there; they lie in a forgotten corner of Kahurangi National Park, north of the Kohaihai River and south of the Heaphy Track. Access to the Downs is awkward, and there's only one old overgrown route called the McNabb Track on the Bellbird Ridge that leads onto the northern part of the

Downs. The appeal of the area is its remoteness, and being unable to find anyone who had been there made it seem all the more attractive. I was naive enough to not to be discouraged by the scrub wall, which, as the map insistently told me, seems to surround the Gunner Downs on all sides.

For some inscrutable reason I had told John Madgwick I would pick him up at four in the morning. Of course I overslept and got there about five, and we drove from Christchurch to the start of the Heaphy Track in a vague blur. We went up the lookout track and launched into the most fearful kiekie forest.

This vine grows close to the coast and has wrist-thick stems that form a powerful net of limbs, so that bashing through it is akin to wrestling with some ancient beast. After a pleasant hour or so with this, we broke out into beech forest and followed what I called the 'Kohaihai Ridge', an undulating bush ridge that runs from the coastline into the head of the Oparara River. It was the old deer cullers' route into the Ugly River in the 1940s, and was still marked with tree blazes and over 30 carefully set gin-traps.

After camping beside a tarn in the rustling beech forest, we dropped down to the head of the Oparara River, and without any legal permit inspected the Honeycomb Caves before continuing on under the top Oparara archway. We crossed from the Oparara River through a jumble of sink-holes and ridges that swerved about with no logic, then descended down into the Kohaihai River and reached the foot of a long spur that led up onto the Gunner Downs. This was where we made our mistake, by starting up the spur.

Spurs can make for open and easier travel, but this one didn't, and our progress slowed and stalled. Shortly after leaving the river we met the scrub belt, which was a thick entwined tangle of alpine totara, fuchsia, mingimingi, turpentine, flax, mountain neinei and every bloody thing God had created. On my map I wrote these terse route notes: at 750 metres 'very slow scrub', at 900 metres 'thick scrub', at 1100 metres 'hard going'. According to my journal the next 300 metres took three hours, and we progressed into an alien-like forest which was so dense that a mat of moss had formed on the top branches in the mistaken belief that this was the ground. We alternatively struggled over this false mossy 'ground', balancing precariously on branches, or went down to the real ground and tried to grovel underneath the scrub.

We were often reduced to ripping off branches to make a tiny hole, just big enough to push a pack through and follow behind. Travel went from 30 vertical metres in ten minutes to 30 vertical metres an hour, but we were never completely baulked. We tried crawling sideways, or scrambling over the top of shrubs. We wriggled and swore, then when that did not work we crept and cursed. As long as we could stand or crouch, break branches and straddle bushes we were able to thrash along by sheer bloody-mindedness. The stuff wasn't impenetrable, though it came damn close, but the prospect of retreat was too painful to think about. John said he was enjoying it, but I thought he was just being ironic.

After four hours struggling up the spur, we met with gratitude the leatherwood and deep tussocks on the downs. A thick mist had settled on the plateau, and we picked our way over it like dishevelled ghosts: there was no track, no water, no sound. Mist coalesced into drizzle, the gouges from the scrub bash got sore and our dry throats ached. We got lost for a while and wandered in foggy basins under Mt Barr, until, just in time and just on dusk, we stumbled across a line of tree blazes, an old hunters' rock bivouac and a small rivulet.

It was dark by the time we lit a fire and drank our billy tea, in a state of something like blissful shock. We counted the scratches and compared notes.

John remarked, 'I've been in worse.'

To which I replied heatedly, 'You must be bloody joking.'

After a long careful pause, a snap of biscuit and a sup of tea, he replied thoughtfully, 'I was.'

Lake Grave

The Light and the Dark are two rivers tucked in behind the Milford Track, first explored by Europeans in January 1905 by a party consisting of W. G. Grave, T. H. 'Oilskin' Hunter, Alf Grenfell and Smith—'a new man'. They went from Worsley River to Sutherland Sound and returned the same way, and had a horrible time, but perhaps that was to be expected.

This remote area was one of the last parts of New Zealand to be explored, and for obvious reasons. The mountains are classically steep and U-shaped, with severe bluffs on both sides of the valleys, and rivers that tend to be either gorges or swamps. There are no tracks, just dense rotting bush and a very high rainfall. Typical of Fiordland, there are few places to camp, and no rest from the sandflies when you do. The area demands extreme bush bashing, with almost every ounce of pleasure squeezed out of the experience.

I have not visited either the Light or the Dark, and having read the stories cannot say I am that keen to go. This account of negotiating Lake Grave is by Penny Hazard, partly based on her account in the Auckland University Tramping Club's magazine *Footprints* (1983), and partly on her own recollections. The other members were Simon Bridger and Chris Peryer, and they had first travelled up the Worsley River over the pass into the Dark River.

11 February 1983
The Dark valley has certainly been appropriately named. We had a long hard day

down to the southern tip of Lake Grave. Massive windfalls and thick bush on moraine, bogs and bluffs hindered progress. For most of the day we could see our destination, six map squares away [about five kilometres], yet it took ten hours of grovelling to get there. It is so difficult to estimate tramping time in Fiordland. It was a relief on nightfall to reach an old campsite mentioned in Moir's Guide. This is occasionally used by hunters and fishermen who have been dropped in by float planes.

12 February

Undeterred by mist clad hills and rain, we set off for the sidle around the western side of Lake Grave. Two slips extending 1000 feet (300 m) up from the lake edge presented immediate problems. We had heard of one party successfully crossing them near the lake edge, so thought we would follow their approach. Huge bluffs, dense bush and boulders made progress next to impossible. We were relying largely

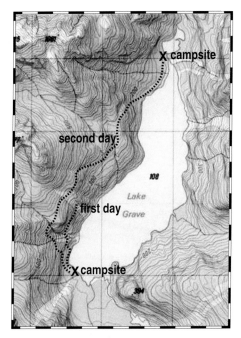

Lake Grave

on ferns as handholds up very steep slopes, and at one stage we managed to lead ourselves up a slimy waterfall chute, only to find we were stuck and had to back-track. The likelihood of an unplanned hydro-slide into the lake, some 1000 feet (300 m) below, was not a nice thought.

Five and a half hours later, we were only half a mile (1 km) horizontally from where we had set off that morning! We decided it was best to retreat, for to camp in that terrain was impossible and there were insufficient daylight hours left to reach the other end of the lake.

Half a day pit bashing was a relief, and rain continued while we amused ourselves counting sandflies in our dinner. We totalled 175 in the billy, and the individual bowl contest was won with 44. We were never able to relax until nightfall, when the sandflies disappeared. Meal times were a chore, each spoonful sabotaged by inhaling or swallowing the black bastards.

13 February

Sleep had been restless, with a combination of achey limbs, abrasions and the anxiety of facing Lake Grave again. But at least the weather was perfect.

This was probably my hardest tramping day ever. It took us ten and a half hours to cover the three kilometres around Lake Grave. Not only was it physical exertion, but also mental. We could never let our minds relax or thoughts wander, because of the chance of falling down a hole, or slipping off a rotten log. Every footstep had to count.

This time, we went even higher, and sidled 1500 feet (500 m) above the lake to avoid the slips and chutes. The descent was interesting, for we could never be quite sure if we were going to be bluffed or not, and the lake shore also posed problems. The steep bush sides would meet deep water immediately, so there was no natural gravel edge around the lake to walk on. We had to scramble along, hoping not to get bluffed again. By this stage, the stress and strain was showing, everyone tired and speaking little.

On finally reaching a campsite at the end of the lake, we still could not properly rest, until daylight had gone and taken the sandflies with it. Exhausted, but contented, we at last could sit back and watch the memorable evening light. A craggy mountain range at the southern end of Lake Grave was silhouetted in the twilight *band reflected perfectly in the glass lake. This beauty, combined with the extraordinary challenge of the lake sidle, depicts the Fiordland I know.*

Salmon Creek Biv

Logbook Entry, Salmon Creek Biv
10 June 2000, Frank King, Honora Renwick.
Giving the track the regulation forestry cut. Spent two days finishing off the track. I guess what we've done will be growing over in about five years. Now let me put this bluntly—I know that most of the people who put on a pack and boots and travel the back-country think they are tough and resourceful. The truth is for two generations you have been a bunch of weak-kneed faggots who grizzle and whine for nanny government to make it easy for you. Time to grow up and do a bit yourselves. Fellahs—it's not hard.

Salmon Creek Biv is deep in the beech forest of lower Salmon Creek, behind Black Hill in Oxford Forest. Throughout the 1990s Frank King and Honora Renwick visited the biv regularly and maintained the track by their own efforts, and there are many people in other mountain areas who do much the same without any acknowledgement.

Grim day at rock biv; from left Steve Kennedy, Sven Brabyn, Mark Pickering.
(Photo: Tom Halliburton).

CHAPTER FOUR

CANTERBURY GREYWACKE

Arthur's Pass National Park has been unkindly compared to a pile of rubble, and sometimes you feel as if the Canterbury mountain landscape should be called 'grey unlimited'. But if you were a poor student living in Christchurch in the 1980s, without a car and dependent on the railway, then this was the landscape you had to work with.

The Inuit people of the Arctic are reputed to have 20 words for snow, and the English undoubtedly have 20 expressions for rain, but Canterbury trampers have an extensive and expressive language for rock: gravel riverbeds, stony gullies, boulder fields, scree slopes, rock guts, slabs, weetbix, bluffs, shingle-slides, eroded cliffs, and so on and so forth.

In one *Canterbury Mountaineering Journal* the rock-climbing safety instructor sagely advised that if you want to make sure you have a good hold on a solid piece of Canterbury rock, just take it out and have a look at it. But make sure you put it back firmly, so the next person can use it.

But you get fond of the stuff you have in your own backyard, and the Canterbury beech forests, eroded tops and braided rivers still figure largely in my memories of tramping 20 years ago. They were cheap to get to and big enough to take seriously. Some people died in them, but most of us came back blistered or bedraggled, having either conquered a peak or been sent back with our tails between our legs.

The following stories all have some connection with the Canterbury back country, and cast an affectionate glance at the enthusiasm and risks with which we engaged those mountains.

Well Trained

These days it seems faintly ridiculous that a 50-ton assemblage of locomotive and clanking carriages would grind to a halt in the middle of nowhere, just to drop off a few trampers. But for generations of Christchurch trampers from the 1930s to the 1980s, this was the only way to get from town into the Arthur's Pass National Park bush, and certainly the cheapest. The 'stations' included such well-known travelling hot-spots as Mt White Bridge, Cora Lynn, Bealey Bridge and Aickens.

The Friday night railcar to Greymouth would be jammed with people, and it used to be chaos, with packs thrown on and 60 or 70 trampers from different Christchurch clubs milling around, stuffing fish and chips into their mouths and getting ice-axes stuck in the doorways. The ticket collector invariably got some supplemental wages by a 'stand-up fee' from trampers without seats.

There was a big rush to the pie stop at Springfield, then the railcar wound tediously through the Waimakariri River gorge, sometimes stopping to let a hunter slip off furtively into the gloom of Staircase Creek.

By the time we arrived at Mt White Bridge, which was the main access for the Hawdon and Andrews Rivers, it was pitch black, and trampers milled around the luggage compartment, grabbed their packs and headed across the bridge and down the shingle road to the mountains, their torches jiggling like demented glow-worms.

There was a stop at Bealey Bridge for the Mingha-Deception, Crow

River and Waimakariri Col trips, then it was on to Arthur's Pass and through the tunnel to Aickens for drop-offs for the Taramakau River trips up over Harper Pass. Then the whole process was reversed on Sunday night, and, if it was risky getting dropped off, then it was a lot more exciting getting back on. One story I particularly like was told to me by my flatmate and his girlfriend in about 1982.

They had booked the train to stop on Sunday night at Aickens Halt, where there's a small grotty wayside shelter, having just come down the Taramakau River from Harper Pass. It was seven o'clock on a winter evening, pitch black and drizzling, and their last torch battery was fading fast. As the railcar approached, they wiggled their pathetic torch, flapped their arms and yelled, although they believed the yelling was for their psychological benefit only. The train thundered up and predictably roared past. They stared in disbelief, cursing New Zealand

Packs off the railcar at Bealey Bridge, Arthur's Pass.

Railways and all its multitudinous workforce, and stood with pain on their faces as the rain pelted against their parkas. Then, with a dramatic pause and a great grinding of brakes and zinging sparks, the train came to a staggering halt some 100 metres away. My flatmate and his girl-friend's curses immediately turned to cries of 'Hooray for New Zealand Railways and their noble staff,' as they grabbed their packs and started to run towards the train.

But New Zealand Railways had not done with them yet. Unbe-lievably, they heard the train start again, its wheels turning and hooter sounding, as if to move off again. At this point my flatmate lost his temper, threw his pack down in disgust on the railtracks and was just about to repeat his curse against New Zealand Railways and all its mal-odorous staff when he abruptly realised that the railcar was reversing!

Slowly it groaned backwards, all 50 tons of it, to the little shelter, where the guard's door banged open throwing a square patch of light on the stunned trampers.

'Nearly missed yer, eh!'

The guard cheerfully slung on the packs and hauled the humbled trampers aboard. Pretty good service for $8.50 return.

Up the Waimak

If it's a grey day, with southerly cloud dulling the mountains, and the wind carrying that special kind of aggravating cold that seems to gnaw into your marrow, then trudging up the Waimakariri River is about as much fun as picking the boss's nose. And why would you go any-way? The riverbed is corrugated with confusing channels, the stones bleached white by silt and interrupted by clumps of islands covered with scabby weed.

But fortunately not every day is like that in the Waimak. In summer the river can shimmer, and the braids of water interlace into myriads of pretty silver ribbons that any young girl would covet. As you swing back and forth across the hot valley you often surprise a pair of paradise ducks that persistently honk at you in the blue air. On these days the river stones twitch with life: a hare bolts from his hiding place and dotterels chatter anxiously as you drift near their nest. As the mountains slide past you glimpse waterfalls that gush with maidenly restraint, well hidden by the cloak of beech forest, and you admire peaks that in your imagination you might one day climb.

The tramp up the Waimak is the quintessential Canterbury journey. It's a tramp so many have done so often: leaving Klondyke Corner and walking into the broad river valley to experience whatever emotions the mountains have. I have vowed several times never to grind up this river again, but every time I break my promise because of one simple fact—the Waimak leads somewhere.

To the Crow River perhaps, and under the dark face of Rolleston. Or via the Jordan and Anti-Crow Rivers over low saddles into the Avoca valley. Or perhaps when you get to the top forks you will turn left, cross the stodgy semolina current of the White River and climb up to Barker Hut and onto Mt Murchison, at 2408 metres the high peak of Arthur's Pass National Park. Turn right at the forks and a track skedaddles up past the gorge and arrives at the battered tin shed at Waimak Falls. Then you can carry on to the Waimakariri Col, which leads into the charmless scree guts of the Rolleston River.

Rather than turning left or right, you could slip straight ahead into the weaselly little Tapoi-iti River which rattles up to Harman Pass. This is the first notable benchmark on the famous Three Pass Trip, which is actually four passes, but no one counts the Styx Saddle when put alongside Whitehorn Pass and Browning Pass.

In rain or storm or sunshine it always seems to take three hours to get up the Waimak from Klondyke Corner to Carrington Hut. When I was young I just blasted across the shingle, taking a perverse pride in taking a line of sight onto a mountain and mangling a dead straight course across whatever channel or gully got in my way. My feet hurt as I crunched along but I didn't care. Slightly older now, I do care and choose to include some of the river's ephemeral islands, and enjoy the flat turf as a relief from the impact of stones. Utilising either the young or old version, it still seems to take three hours.

Once I found a V8 cylinder block poking out of the gravel, and was told that people used to drive cars to self-destruction up the Waimak, just for fun. Oystercatchers have attacked me, and I have found horribly bloated salmon and trout thrashing about in their death throes as they ejected their milky eggs into the clear water.

I never know which one of the Waimak's moods is the best one, but I know which ones I like. I don't enjoy the hot swirling dust of summer, or the nor'westers that swell over the passes and muzzle down the valleys like an old snuffly dog. I do like the sensuous light of an autumn evening that illuminates the hills as if someone had smeared honey on them. I also enjoy the result of an early winter snowfall, as it drapes tidily down the mountainsides like a washerwoman's well-organised sheets. On a clear June day thick frost crackles underfoot, but just a hint of sun loosens the river stones again and they dribble down into the rushing water, as the whole shebang has been dribbling for millions of years.

The Waimak is not many people's favourite place, but it is well-favoured with routes and opportunities, and I suppose the next generation will have to put up with the same three-hour slog as I did. Despite disparaging it, in hindsight I've probably had more pleasure than pain from this valley, though I still find it inexplicable when I find myself, as I certainly shall, going up the Waimak.

A Tragic Tale

Let me tell you a tragic story—a story where nobody died or was injured, apart from a little humiliating soul damage. This tragic tramp is simply one that turned to custard: comical, frustrating, sticky mountain custard. It's a story of four university friends in 1981 having a gruesome week in the hills and getting a good laugh out of it—at least in retrospect.

It was my first Garden of Eden trip, something I had been looking forward to for months. My flatmate Tony was getting married that weekend, and seemed miffed that I should have turned his wedding invitation down for the Garden of Eden. He'd never heard of it. I patiently explained it was a real earthly paradise, an ice field lying at about 2300 metres in the heart of the Southern Alps.

'You're welcome to it,' he sniffed, 'the only ice I want is in the champagne bucket.'

Taking no notice of the weather forecast, we all crushed into Tom Halliburton's Land Rover, drove up the Rangitata River road and drove round the back of Erewhon homestead to face our first obstacle, the Clyde River. The others on the trip were Sven Brabyn and Steve Kennedy, and we had talked over our strategy on the way, agreeing that we should get out and inspect the river carefully to find the best vehicle fording point. We went down to the river bank and Tom planted his boot.

Even to my inexpert eye he apparently chose the deepest part, and we drove into the water with a rush of spray and steam over the bonnet. Steve and I were trapped in the back with water surging up to the doorwells, lurching and rolling sickeningly over the river boulders. For several seconds I thought we were going to tip, but somehow the Land Rover found some rock underneath, and with a triumphant roar scrambled out of the other side, where Tom announced beaming, 'I've never done that before!'

As we lumbered and lurched up the river bed we got a flat tyre and changed it, but with no more spares left in the cupboard I felt uneasy. We probably broke the first of several U-bolts at this point, though being mechanically illiterate, I was blissfully unaware of the significance of this. We came to a stop near Armada Bluff, then it was a good day's slog up to McCoy Hut—each of us laden with ice-axe, crampons and a snow shovel—as the cloud started to boil over the main divide. Next morning we roped across Frances Creek, never an easy crossing when

Land Rover stuck in the Clyde River.

it is discoloured with glacial 'flour', and by the time we were walking up Campbell Creek to the foot of the glacier it was raining steadily. Shortly someone found a large rock, which he confidently pronounced 'a rock biv'.

It wasn't. This rock had only a small overhang and precious little space underneath. It was exposed to the wind, and even stringing up a fly did not make it comfortable. But we had no choice as it was raining steadily, and to attempt Perth Col would have been hopeless under the circumstances.

We spent two miserable nights in the rock biv while the weather got worse and the rivers roared. Sven started to dig a 'grave' under the rock and gradually squeezed himself and his pit into it, where he stayed nice and comfy. Tom and I struggled to cover ourselves with flys and tents but only got wetter. Steve, who did not want to get his precious sleeping bag damp, roamed around outside for two nights in his down jacket, crouching under small dry overhangs. We prayed for a clearance, but all we got was more rain. The rivers grew more discoloured, then grey, then brown, then swelled over the banks and roared through our dreams.

On the morning after the second miserable night we gave up and decided it was time to escape—but would the mountains let us go? Because we could no longer cross Frances Creek, we bashed high down the true right bank of the Clyde for some six hours to Watchdog Hut. It rained all the way, a sullen, solid rain that saturated our clothes and mental processes, so that all we wanted to do was keep our boots pounding on the stones till we reached the hut.

It was a tremendous relief to sprint madly to the doorway. There were dry bunks for all and food in the cupboard, so we set about the task of dismembering our wet packs and drying out. Steve, who had spent three tortuous days trying to keep his sleeping bag dry, pulled it out, only for a flush of water to empty out of it onto the hut floor. This kept us amused for days.

We had a rest day to dry out gear, and the day after (but too late for us) came the southerly clearance. We had to climb over Armada

Bluff because the river was still too high, and painfully learnt the reason for its name—a host of spaniards. We got to the Land Rover and headed despondently back as the sun played brilliantly on the distant peaks. Tom revved up the engine angrily and belted across the river bed straight into a thick sandy pond, where the Land Rover gurgled miserably and sank up to the axles. Our day was getting worse.

Tom got out the winch and we dug a huge hole, buried the useless spare tyre as an anchor, winched the Land Rover out and proceeded fatalistically to the banks of the mighty Clyde River. After four days of rain it looked hopeless.

Still, we put Steve on a rope to test the river, but as he came back rather wet we trundled around and slept another frustrated night in a hayshed, with the blue sky mocking our efforts to escape. After waiting another twelve hours for the river to drop, we now felt that we had a chance to get out and, after much exploring of the river braids, at about noon on the seventh day we got across and were free.

Not quite. A quick check underneath showed that the number of broken U-bolts had increased to three. These particular bolts attach the springs to the axle, and we needed a full set of front U-bolts to steer the Land Rover. Cleverly, Tom had brought spares, but it took some hours of hacksawing in hot weather to get the old bolts off, swap them around and put the new ones on. Still with one U-bolt busted we crept slowly into the sunset of the seventh day. Back home late that night I found a postcard from my flatmate, who was having his honeymoon in Fiji. 'Wish you were here,' he wrote. Bastard.

The Imperial Treasures of Smith's Emporium

In Christchurch there is (or was) a famous second-hand bookshop called Smith's. It's a rabbit warren of several storeys with a labyrinth of shelving that fills all the space between the floor and the ceiling. The smell is woody and corrupt, the silence thick. Second-hand bookshops are, I suppose, a sort of graveyard, where an author's ambitions and vanity are finally laid to rest. Poets in that dusty corner, essayists there—tramping guidebooks in that cardboard box, Mr Pickering.

Many years ago I was fossicking in Smith's when I came across a carton of old inch-to-the-mile maps. I asked how much they were, but the shop owner looked uninterested: I could have them for 50 cents each, or take the lot for $20. I bargained him down to $15 and went home with my treasures. Most dated from the 1950s and 1960s, but there were also linen maps from the 1940s, particularly of the top half of the South Island.

Farewell Spit 1945, Matiri 1943, Saxton 1945: these were the first edition maps of the inch-to-the-mile series. Printed on heavy linen paper and titled *Provisional 1 mile series*, many had only half- or quarter-completed contour lines, which made them look rather odd, as if someone had placed large red ink thumbprints at random on the sheet. Contours were only possible with the development of accurate aerial photography, which was still in its infancy in the early 1940s, and probably at that time the planes were needed for more pressing matters.

Where there was a lack of detail on the maps, instructions were printed, which may or may not have been useful: *Saxton S34* 'Bare rocky faces and shingle slides snow covered four to six months of the year'; *Murchison S32* 'steep slopes covered with birch bush', 'fairly even snow grass tops' and 'steep broken birch bush partly milled, lower slopes flat spurs and deep gullies'. 'Birch' was the then universal description for beech forest.

On all the early maps the text was carefully seriffed, and the original master must have been handwritten in a fine, exact hand. Drawing and numbering the contours would have needed patience and fortitude, and the unknown scribes usually indicated their work by marking their initials discreetly at the bottom of the sheet 'LRC 1943' or 'TPM 1945'. Sometime in the 1950s handwriting gave way to printing; more colours and better shading were added, and with the completion of aerial photography, most contours included. There was still the occasional blip: the 1965 (first edition) *S150 Mossburn* map shows a small portion of the Takitimu Mountains as a blank, with the helpful note: 'Area obscured by cloud'.

The ambitious scheme to map all of New Zealand on the inch-to-the-mile grid, and establish 100-foot contours for every part of the landscape, took over 40 years to complete. The first maps appeared in the early 1940s, and the last map, *S75 Aspiring*, in March 1976. This was about three months too late for our Christmas tramping trip, but the trip leader had managed at great effort to get a photocopy of an early draft, so we were not completely mapless.

Shortly afterwards it was announced that the imperial measurements were to be replaced by metric measurements, and they were going to do the whole thing all over again. They never did get around to making inch-to-the-mile maps of Stewart Island. By 1998 the metric map system was also completed, in less than 25 years, and within two more years the government (in a most unusual act) returned the copyright to the people of New Zealand, and the maps were duly scanned and digitised for compact discs.

By the late 1990s the Department of Lands and Survey was lumbered with a large number of old inch-to-the-mile maps which had been superseded by the metric series, which were not necessarily more reliable, but at least newer. After the Department had exhausted the retail possibilities of selling the old maps they decided to turn them into envelopes, and (incredibly) shopping bags. I still have one, *Otorohanga N74*, folded crisply and with two handles—perfect for carrying maps!

This little ditty was found in the Auckland University Tramping Club *Footprints* magazine, but is possibly of Scottish origin.

A map has many uses, we are told
It traces tracks, and marks the bridges
Defines the contour lines on the ridges
It will unfold, then tightly rolled
Can massacre the bloody midges.

Avalanche!

This account was written by Kirsty Woods who, with Rob Delamore, Jonathan Jull and Fraser McLaughlan, planned to climb Mt Rolleston at Arthur's Pass on a winter weekend in 1989.

It was mid-term break and we were spending a few days at Rob's family bach at Arthur's Pass. Most of our group were keen to hug the fire, but Rob, Fraser and Jonathan were aiming to climb Mt Rolleston if the weather was clear, and I decided that I would go along.

I remember we left in cold, clear conditions though the wind was up. We started up the Bealey Valley, intending to climb via the Bealey Slide and Goldney Ridge. I was feeling a bit clumsy and it took me a while to get into the rhythm of things. Some other friends were doing a more relaxing trip on the West Coast, and as we ground up the hill I wondered if it wouldn't have been more sensible to have done that instead.

I warmed up on the Bealey Slide and started looking around. On the lower slopes the snow was low but patchy. Above us to the left were some small bluffs, and below them, but quite a distance to the left of us, was a narrow column of avalanche debris. I don't think any of us gave it much thought at the time.

We worked our way across a wide patch of crusty snow and rock, and I remember feeling a bit uncomfortable as I wasn't as fit as the others. The higher we climbed the colder the wind became, so I took off my helmet to put on my hat. Fraser and Rob were up ahead, and Jonathan stayed at the back with me.

Eventually we reached a narrow gut above the small bluff that I'd noticed earlier. The snow conditions had changed from a thin crust to deep drifts, like piles of tiny particles of polystyrene, and I was wading in the gut, thigh-deep in snow. I could see that Rob and Fraser were starting to make their way onto what looked like firmer ground ahead.

I heard a crack. The snow beneath my feet moved and before I knew it I was on my back, enveloped in snow and speeding down head first. I couldn't see anything and as I gathered speed I could feel myself being launched into the air. I hit the ground again and sped on without being able to see a thing. At one point I felt the snow conveyor belt slow down and saw a bit of blue sky, but then it was all whiteness and I was off again. It's hard to describe what went through my mind, but a whole lot of thoughts were scrambled together:

'There are big bluffs somewhere around here and any minute now I'll be gone. How dumb, why didn't we think about avalanches? Why didn't I go to the West Coast instead? What about my family and friends? Won't they miss me? Will they be angry?'

I tried to wrestle myself around the other way, remembering some sort of advice about swimming with the avalanche, but I had no idea where I was and couldn't help thinking about the bluffs and how they'd be getting pretty close. I wasn't too keen to swim over a bluff, and anyhow I still couldn't turn over.

I can't say how long it took. It seemed like ages but was probably only twenty to thirty seconds. Just when I thought I was about to disappear for good, I slowed down again and was able to sit up out of the snow, which had spread right out as the slope flattened out.

I was way over to the left of the route we'd taken up the slope. The large bluffs I'd imagined were still a long way off. Two tiny dots were running down towards me, and Jonathan was further down the slope, shaken and his face covered in blood. His glasses had come off and one of the lenses had made a deep cut between the top of his nose and his eye. His ice-axe had cut gashes in his parka and through three layers of clothes underneath. My ice-axe had made a cut in the side of my knee, but I couldn't feel anything and the ice-axe was nowhere to be seen. Breathing felt weird; both of us felt as though our lungs were full of snow.

Rob and Fraser made their way down to us as we got to grips with what had happened, and we returned slowly to Arthur's Pass village and back to Rob's bach.

Jonathan Jull, a few hours after the avalanche. (Kirsty Woods)

The rest of the weekend was spent discovering extra scratches and piecing together our stories, and I resolved to take more care in future.

The following summer, when Rob and Jonathan were up at Arthur's Pass for the holidays, they went for a walk near where we had climbed and found my ice-axe on the rocks under the small bluff. These days I keep the ice-axe in the attic as a souvenir of that day on the Bealey Slide.

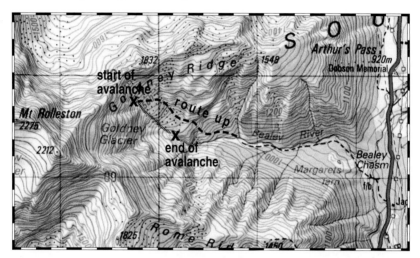

Site of Avalanche

CHAPTER FIVE

ELEMENTS

It is often remarked by people who go into the outdoors that they want to 'get away from it all', or 'get back to nature'. It's an awkward way to express a desire to lead a more elemental life and to experience places where other people are scant on the ground, and where the night is truly dark. Where fire is essential and personal, and starlight is untrammelled. Where there are opportunities to experience silences that are so deep, and sometimes so absolute, that on occasion all you can hear is the roaring of blood in your own ears.

Humans by and large are a companionable species, and we live in comfortable homes in large social groups of families and friends. Our clock-regulated patterns of life are both reassuring and pleasant. More than that, witnessing the birth of your child is as profound an experience as anyone could wish for—why would you want more?

Civilisation has availed us of so many benefits that it seems perverse to reject them for the uncertain joys of mountains. So it will always be only a few people who, for a brief time, prefer to endure a level of discomfort simply for the pleasure of feeling closer to the elements. It is not something that is easy to explain or justify, and the following chapters probably do not do it very well.

Wilderness

Anyone who lies on their back in the mountains at night and stares up at the starlit heavens knows immediately that on this planet there is no such thing as wilderness anymore. No untouched worlds.

Satellites cross the hemispheres, and seeds from one continent are planted in another. Tourists transfer (accidentally or deliberately) insects, microbes, pollen, attitudes. You will not find a speck of land on this planet that humans have not made some impact upon, and even the atmosphere itself is laden with human scent: it carries minute traces of radioactive elements from the atomic bombs that were exploded in test series for over 30 years. Indeed, our children's bodies carry these same trace elements.

In the classic 1940s western film *The Man Who Shot Liberty Valance*, the very last scene is set on a train travelling across the once desert landscape. The wife (Vera Miles) turns eagerly to the husband (James Stewart) and says, 'Look out there, once this was a wilderness, now it's a garden.' The point being made is that wilderness is anti-human and must be tamed. 'Go forth and multiply' was the biblical instruction to create a literal Garden of Eden out of this promised planet.

In the 1850s the word 'wilderness' in New Zealand meant a wasteland: an uncultivated and in a sense infertile land where no human being could exist. Numerous early writers referred to the mountains as 'a useless wilderness' or 'a barren wilderness'. The early colonists tried to create 'a productive land' and 'a fertile land'.

But 150 years later we have turned these concepts on their heads so that today we view wilderness as land untainted by human development and therefore 'natural', 'untrampled', and (it gets confusing) even as a 'garden' or 'nature's garden'. Some people even think of wilderness as fertile and healthy, in contrast to barren and unhealthy cities.

Wilderness, whatever it may be, is now in short supply, and humans, being a contrary species, have therefore begun to place a value on it. They have even gone one step further and turned it into a commodity, and, perversely, now make a profit out of something that they hitherto felt was so manifestly unproductive. Hotels and roads are built so the wilderness can be viewed. Books, calendars, postcards and brochures sell poetic wilderness concepts to visitors that would have been curses on the lips of the pioneers—untouched, wild, remote, barren, primeval. Scenic flights, helicopter landings and guided walks all exploit the wilderness for profit, and there are remote and expensive hotels in wild parts of New Zealand which visitors access in environmentally unfriendly vehicles such as planes and cars to be assured that they have arrived in an unspoilt environment called 'wilderness'.

Vivian Pybus and Nic Bishop in a snowstorm on Lagoon Saddle.

Of course it's silly. The Garden of Eden exists in the mind only, so if there is no such thing as wilderness, what are we protecting with all these remote areas and national parks?

For the recreational user, the answer is choice. Wilderness provides the opportunity to live crudely and basically; to exist on your wits and manage your immediate environment as if your life depended on it; to play at being an explorer or a hunter-gatherer, and to get a whiff of the times when lighting a fire was deadly serious, and killing your meal literally a matter of life and death. In that sense tramping is deeply nostalgic—an escape from urban reality. But hardly a very good escape, especially if you carry a GPS, a cell phone and an emergency locater beacon.

But perhaps instead of talking of wilderness we should talk of remoteness. When people say 'they want to get away from it all', perhaps all they mean is they want to put a little distance between themselves and the rest of the frantic world, at least for a while. So in that sense there is value in trying to preserve certain corners of the earth where some people can have an escape, because it would be terrible if there was no choice. If there was no escape.

If I had to choose a particular portion of wilderness over another then I would choose Marks Flat in South Westland. There are many more places in Fiordland or the Olivine Mountains that are harder to get to, and there are places with more evocative names like the Forgotten River, or the Bowels of the Earth, or the Valley of Darkness, but there are few places where remoteness comes with such an encompassing sense of peace. The scale of scenery is breathtaking, yet unthreatening. You don't feel imprisoned at Marks Flat, you feel you have reached a sanctuary.

The flat is two kilometres long and one kilometre wide. Small creeks wriggle through the alpine tussocks like shiny snakes caught out in the open, and after rain the wetland area becomes a series of ponds, tinged red with the waterweed. On the north side of the flat is Mt Hooker, some 2000 metres of rock slabs and ice escarpments that make your eyes squint as you follow the spur lines to the invisible summit. On the south side of the flat is Kea Cliffs, a 300-metre wall of awesome rock, and beyond that the Solution Range.

At the western end of the flat is a mess of boulders that have created any number of plausible rock bivs, but the best rock biv is in the

Jan Simmons looking towards Marks Flat.

middle of the flat. Every one of these giant boulders has crumbled off the bare-faced sides of Mt Hooker, and some are still falling. To the east there is Lower Otoko Pass, squashed between Mt Hooker on one side and the enormous snow dome of Mt Dechen on the other.

All this magnificence does not come cheaply, and Marks Flat is not an easy place to reach by foot. It sits at the head of the Clarke River, a tributary of the great Landsborough River, so if you want to gain access to the Clarke you have to first cross the Landsborough, the mightiest of the South Westland rivers. Once this little difficulty is overcome you have about 15 kilometres of uncertain river travel up the Clarke past two deep gorges before you reach Monro Flat, at which point you either struggle up Saddle Creek or follow the *Moir's Guide* instructions and sneak around the base of Kea Cliffs and into the haven of Marks Flat. Depending on weather and river crossings, allow for at least two to three days travel.

An alternative to the Clarke is to go up the Otoko River. You start from the Paringa road bridge and follow the Paringa for half a day till you reach its confluence with the Otoko. After a few kilometres of easy travel you begin a 15-kilometre struggle with West Coast boulders the size of houses, pleasantly smothered with thick bush. All in all allow for two days from the road to the head of the Otoko, and a day crossing rock fields over Lower Otoko Pass and brushing past a bluff or two down to Marks Flat.

Then there's the Landsborough access. A jolly jaunt of 25 kilometres from the road end, crossing the river if possible, otherwise both Strutts Bluff and Harper Bluff may prove troublesome, as will the long boulder bash on the true left. At Creswicke or Toetoe Flat you climb over 1000 metres to the top of the Solution Range and past several gorgeous tarns to a full frontal eye-stopping view of Mt Hooker that you will never forget. With heavy packs it hardly seems possible in less than three days.

Some smart trampers consider the Paringa River option, which has the advantage of a good track up to Tunnel Creek Hut, then a 1000 metre gut buster climb to a rock biv that has one of the finest views on the West Coast. The route then climbs over a steepish unnamed pass and descends the McCullaugh Creek, which gets slower and slower in tangled bush down to Monro Flat in the Clarke River. From there it's a half day on to Marks Flat. A cunning route, but still two and a half hard days.

So it takes three days to get to Marks Flat, one day to rest, and another three days to get out. There's a week gone—but what a week. The second time I went there (in 1985) we came down the Landsborough River, groaned up onto the Solution Range, and then continued out via the Paringa River. The trip went swimmingly, with nigh perfect weather, but when we got to Marks Flat—where was the food drop?

I had rung the helicopter pilot, James Scott, months beforehand to ask how much a drop there would be.

'What's it worth to yer?' was his reply.

I was not expecting it to be put like that. I said we'd come down and discuss it. So about three weeks later Nick Miller, Jan Simmons, Nic Bishop and I trundled down to South Westland, and found the chopper pilot's $4000 house beside his $100,000 machine (these are 1980s' prices). We wanted a food drop by the rock biv at Marks Flat, so how much would it be?

'What's it worth to yer?' Scottie asked.

Oh no, not again. We put off the decision and decided to discuss it on the way out. We gave him our sealed tubs and repeated nervously, 'By the rock biv, OK?' He just sneered.

After a glorious week of fine weather we cruised over the Solution Range and dropped down to the isolated piece of perfection that is Marks Flat. The rock biv was clearly marked on all our maps, near the outlet at the lower end of the flat. We found it quite quickly, no problem there. There was a big cairn on top of it, luring trampers towards a disappointment because it was a cramped, gloomy hole.

But where was the food? We scouted around the outside for 20 minutes, then spread the search wider. It was quite a jumble of rocks, which had obviously at some time peeled off Kea Cliffs and stacked themselves in a thorough muddle. We searched unperturbed for a while and found two more rock bivs. Still no food. Hmmm … it was time for a conference.

For the next two hours we searched systematically, slowly and carefully examining every likely and unlikely nook and cranny. That bloody chopper man and his sardonic smile! We had 100 grams of rice, a couple of soup packets, and some odd bits of cracker and chocolate stashed away, which, perish the thought, might have to last us for days. Marks Flat is one of the more isolated places to starve in, and even with a good hike it couldn't take us less than three days to get out via the Paringa River.

After another hour's searching, we found yet another rock biv, quite high up the slope, but no food. This was getting ridiculous. No matter how many rock bivs we found we could not find the food. However, we were still calm about it; I couldn't believe the pilot had *forgotten*, but I was uneasy for I knew that in South Westland they operate on a different time-scale, so it *might* have slipped his mind.

Eventually someone suggested we try the actual airstrip, and so we grabbed our packs and fanned off across the flat. I munched on quite a feed of snowberries, as it rather looked as if I would need to eat as many of them as ... A shout! There were two plastic tubs on the airstrip! Full of food and untouched by the keas. What a relief, but where in tarnation was the rock biv? Had the stupid pilot just dumped them down on any old spot?

'What's that?'

'That bloody large rock over there?'

'Yeah.'

We went and had a look. It was a bloody large rock, house-sized in fact, flat in profile, with one end lifted up and a very comfortable posi underneath. You could stand upright and have a panoramic view of Marks Flat. It obviously wasn't the rock biv marked on the map, but it was by far and away the best (and we'd found just about every one) on the flat. With stomachs full of Christmas pudding and burping on Christmas cheer we were inclined to be contemplative and somewhat forgiving of the chopper pilot as the setting sun beautified our brandy-ripened faces.

But there is an unfinished coda to the story, for we still hadn't paid for the food drop. Back in South Westland, we converged on Scottie's place again. It was late evening and there he was with all his cronies hanging around. How much did he want now?

'What's it worth to yer?'

Oh God, here we went again. A long silence, then I summoned up some resolution and timidly started to suggest, 'Maybe two hun...' But my more economically-minded mate rushed in with a thriftier offer, 'One hundred dollars.'

There was a pause.

'Fifty will do yer.'

Beer money. The helicopter blokes in South Westland have some curious methods.

Days and Nights in the Forest

One November I quit an unpleasant job and left town unpaid, unsettled and upset by civilisation. I needed an antidote, so I hitched down to the Routeburn Track, crossed the main divide and looked down on the smokey ranges of Fiordland, my gaze following the silky serpentine twist of the Hollyford River as it bled down to the sea.

The rain had started by the time I got to Gunns Camp on the Hollyford Road, where Murray Gunn looked me over with an experienced eye, sold me a slab of 'Trampers Soap' (a chunk of Sunlight Soap) and led me to the scruffiest of his huts. For heating and cooking there was a wood burner, and just on evening Murray came out through the pelting rain with a lighted kerosene lamp.

Gunns Camp was an unusual place. There were strange concrete mushrooms on the ground, painted in pinks and blues; and around the huts wandered an old horse called Jane, with the word 'horse' painted in large white letters on her side, one of Murray's many jokes. His museum (the original one, before it burnt down) was a bewildering collection of memorabilia, jokes and junk.

Murray reminded me of a weka with a sharp blood-eye, but over the years I met him several times and gradually began to appreciate his quirky sense of humour. He had lived in the heart of the Hollyford forest all his life, had met Arawhata Bill once, and was contemptuous of John Pascoe. 'Are you a tops man or a valley man?' Pascoe once asked Murray, who imitated Pascoe's cultured tones with well-practised irony.

Murray was keen on history and had a whole swagful of documents and jottings that were going towards 'his book', though I'm still not sure if it's been written. On one occasion when I stayed for a night, I gave Murray a copy of my history book *The Southern Journey*, and this got him marvellously excited. All evening he came shuffling over to my hut with another bit of a journal, and another photocopy of someone else's diary; a virtual cavalcade of history collected through the long twilights of the Hollyford Valley. He was still coming back and forth

Old signpost at Gunns Camp, erected by Murray Gunn (1993).

at midnight, and because I was leaving early the next day the only way I could ever read it all was to stay up all night. I got a headache from the kerosene and my eyes went blurry from trying to decipher Murray's handwriting.

But back to my visit in 1983: the rain was still blattering down when I said goodbye to Murray and plodded down the road to the start of the track. The Hollyford is a weird track for it starts at the end of the Hollyford Road at an altitude of only 100 metres above sea level, and then takes about 40 kilometres to finally reach the surf at Long Reef. That's about three days one way and then three days back: a week of days and nights in the forest.

After Hidden Falls Hut the rain had eased with an encouraging burst of sun, and I stopped to have a brew by the river bank. Fantails were excited by my presence, and I tempted one to land on my out-stretched hand. It brushed my fingers like a nature sprite, and I sat down with a feeling of being blessed. It seems to me that different forests have differing tones of light underneath them: North Island puriri trees soften the air with silver shades, whilst Kaweka kanuka forest makes the light brittle and flighty. Under the massive podocarp forest of the Hol-lyford Valley the sunlight seemed exhausted, as if every clutching branch and tree fern had grabbed a handful of it on the way down, and what remained when it reached the ground settled quietly about my feet more like a memory of sunlight.

But this daydreaming wasn't getting me anywhere. The long swing-bridge across the Pyke River trembled as the full flooded force of the West Coast poured down underneath, and I reached Demon Trail Hut as the heavens opened again. It rained all night, and the next day I got five minutes along the track and was stopped by the boiling fury of a side-creek, so I had to go back to the hut and wait. Two women turned up bedraggled and defeated, moaning about the slimy bush and sticky tracks. But by noon the creek had dropped, and I followed the track as it continued on the Demon Trail, which is a series of stumbles up and down gullies alongside Lake McKerrow. It's a dank and unpleasant section of forest, clinging to the steep lake hillsides with vines and supplejacks that writhe like black snakes. I found an old horseshoe by the lake edge, and it immediately reminded me of the famous rescue tramp by Davy Gunn in 1936.

At the time he was running cattle to Martins Bay, and in the process establishing a tourist operation with huts and pack-horses—the first Hollyford Track in fact. In that year a Fox Moth aeroplane crashed at Big Bay, killing one man and severely injuring four others, including the pilot. After helping the injured, Davy Gunn left the crash site at seven in the evening, rode 15 kilometres to his hut at Martins Bay, then rowed another 15 kilometres up the long Lake McKerrow. Then came the difficult section: a tramp over the Hollyford Track in the dark for 40 kilometres to the road end, where he got out to the nearest telephone at Marian at four in the afternoon, covering the entire distance of 90 kilometres in 20 hours. It was a remarkable journey, and there's still a commemorative plaque to him beside the Milford Road.

Forest on Hollyford Track (2002).

In the museum at Gunns Camp there is a collection of saddles and memorabilia from those days, all exhibits carefully recorded in Murray's dry notes, and it made me realise that here is a man who has lived a whole lifetime under his father's famously muscular shadow, and not always easily.

Back on the Demon Trail I spooked a deer, which panicked and got entangled in an iron latticework of supplejack; round and round it went, getting more furiously entwined, till with a desperate heave it broke free and went off barking madly in the bush. Minutes later I saw a stoat scuttle over the track, carrying its baby in its mouth. I was glad to get to Hokuri Hut and blast along the flat land around the lost settlement of Jamestown. That evening I rigged the fly up under some tall podocarps and experienced that peculiar feeling you sometimes get under large trees, that they become mobile at night and shuffle restlessly on their arthritic roots.

My diary records 'heavy, heavy rain and surface floods' that day through to Martins Bay Hut, and I stumbled over ten or so Fiordland crested penguins as I fossicked for firewood on the stormy shore. Feeling right at the edge of the world I was surprised to find two government track-cutters slashing away at the fern, and I gave them a cup of tea. We talked about the forest and what we'd seen. They'd watched a bush falcon training its young by dropping a piece of carrion meat midair, and cheered on the young bird as it successfully snatched its morsel. One man remarked that he found the forest oppressive at times, and even hated it, yet he'd been coming back to the Hollyford for six years. 'Sap,' he grumbled, 'is what I've got for blood.'

One of my feet was getting sore, so I decided to put my head down and slog out the return journey as quick as I could. I made a half-day march to Hokuri Hut, followed by a full gruesome day on to Hidden Falls. The side-creeks rumbled with brown stew, the lake was grey and unsettled, the forest birds were silent; I couldn't even get a fire going for a brew and had to munch on dry muesli for lunch. It finally ceased raining when I was almost at Hidden Falls Hut.

Inside the hut I found an attractive American woman who seized on me for a conversation. 'You're the first person I've seen all day. This forest is so quiet.'

I should have relished this social opportunity, but I was too tired to make much sense. I shunned her charms, slung up my fly outside on the flats and lit a fire. A large kiwi came rolling around curiously, sniffing at this and that, seemingly repelled and attracted by the flames. It was a memorable moment.

In the morning I hobbled to the carpark and had walked barely 50 metres along the road when out of the bushes a van driven by one of the track workers miraculously appeared. He whisked me to the Milford Sound road, and then another mini-van stopped and immediately took me to Te Anau. This magical mystery ride continued with a sequence of effortless hitching that has never been repeated in my life since. On the Dunedin motorway I stuck out my thumb and two cars pulled over simultaneously. After leaving Hidden Falls Hut that morning I finally crawled into a hayshed on the Moeraki coast and fell into a torpor.

I dreamt of how the accumulation of trivial incidents on the tramp had made such a complete journey. I remembered Davy Gunn and his epic trek, his son Murray proudly and bitterly hoarding an emporium of his father's memories. There was the terrified red deer, the loving stoat, the nosey kiwi; the man who hated forest and the woman who just wanted some company; and the great green forest that swallowed us, hurried us along and pushed us out again, ready for another dose of city life. I have heard of a theory that the reason people feel refreshed by forests is because there is a richer concentration of oxygen within them. I see no reason to doubt it.

Fire

The moment humans gained control of fire must have generated the first great creative outburst of storytelling. For as well as being useful, fire is civilising. Even with stone tools, humans would only have kept away wild beasts with difficulty, but with fire they could build a bonfire at the entrance to their cave and no wild animal would dare face it to attack them.

Once safe, humans could relax and, in the aftermath of a meal of roasted flesh, pass the long winter nights around the comfort of the fire telling stories to amuse and thrill. Fire creates bonds, camaraderie and closeness. The stories would not just be about what might be eaten tomorrow, or what had been eaten today, for although the great mass of people rarely get beyond a practical existence, there would have been others—singers, gleemen, storytellers—with a greater creative instinct who would have invented the fantastic myths and adventures of heroes that satisfy the soul.

Fire freed these stories so they could rise like sparks, catching on dark branches and spiralling up into the stars themselves. This is not too fanciful: all ancient peoples worshipped fire and had their great storytellers. Fire craved constant attention to maintain its existence, and needed special people to ignite it and care for it. Were these people the first priests?

A society with fire would not want to lose it, and those members of nomadic peoples who could always make fire, in whatever place or circumstance, were surely very valuable indeed. You would protect them, shelter them, give them special honours and the best meats; and perhaps these fire-makers invented strange chants and mystic songs to conceal the crude mechanical act of creating fire. They began to grasp their power and insist on strange, ghastly rituals. Fire was worshipped, and so were the fire-makers. In most primitive societies fire always played a central role in ceremonies, and whenever there was fire there were priests and shamans who danced around it, capturing its spirit in order to celebrate the divine, but also to enhance their own powers.

In the modern world fire is still greatly enjoyed, though somewhat frowned upon. In Christchurch on 5 November there is a huge participation in Guy Fawkes Night, and in parks, private gardens and at public displays fireworks erupt well into the night over the whole city. Although bonfires are banned in the city, they still twinkle across the Canterbury plains, evidence of people enjoying fire.

Is this a lingering attachment to a much older custom of bonfires, or bone fires? The Celts considered November the month of the dead, a time when evil spirits roamed the land spreading death and misery. Bonfires were lit on the first day of November to rid the neighbourhood of these beings, to mark the end of the old year and to purify slaughtered animal carcasses in a ritual that was both spiritual and environmentally sound. The practice continued into the Christian era:

> *...in the worship of St John the people made three manner of fires: one was of clean bones and no wood, and that is called a bone fire. Another of clean wood and no bones, and is called a wood fire. And the third is made of wood and bones, and is called St Johns fire.*
> —Festyvall, printed by Wynkyn de Worde in 1515

Poor Guy Fawkes' inadequate attempt in November 1605 to blow up Parliament simply coincided with the bone fire season. A 'guy' was stuck on top, and fireworks were added to the festival.

There was a debate in *New Zealand Geographic* magazine some years ago about the ethical role of fire-making in a tramping context. The primus owners were feeling virtuous that they were helping the planet a little by not burning the precious cargo of kindling on the forest floor. They stated that all the woody detritus is needed by foraging insects and birds and as mulch for the young seedlings.

But primuses are created by fire. The aluminium is wrought from vast factories, consuming huge amounts of material and energy. Petrol and white spirits have been found by digging into the ground at prodigious expense, then successively refined and transported right across the world to wild New Zealand valleys. So all this virtue comes at a price; indeed, primuses are certainly more expensive, less practical and less renewable than simple firewood.

But this is old-fashioned talk from an old codger who still likes to sit by a fire in the evening hills and watch the sparks tumble skywards. I don't doubt that open-air fires will soon be banished from the mountains, and it is disheartening to watch groups of trampers huddled around primuses with a false environmental reluctance to light a fire. Do they know its real worth?

People need fire. It connects us with our past and our ancestors. For millions of years humans have lived and worked with fire and found beside it warmth, solace and sometimes a spiritual presence. Try as we might, our little gods are not winning any battles against the greater materialistic gods, but some things give us a sense of the numinous, and one of those is fire.

Tussock, Rock and Snow

Arawhata Saddle was a difficult pass, we knew that, and for three days and nights the weather had trapped us in Liverpool Biv, a tiny shelter perched on the abyss which was the Matukituki Valley. The wind rattled the hut all day, and Christmas Day dinner in 1979 was a small portion of rice, some packet soups for flavour and four squares of chocolate. The balloons someone brought did not cheer us up. On Boxing Day the bidding in our game of 500 became more extravagant, and only four days into the tramp we were rationing food, the balloons were deflating and we still had to get over the saddle.

Then the weather cleared and eight trampers packed up, bashed through the tussock and rock basin to the foot of the steep snow slopes under the pass, and paused nervously. At this crux there was a moment of comedy.

One man waved his crampons about with the nervous question, 'How do you put these on again?' They were brand-new crampons, but he couldn't work them out at all, which was hardly surprising. The salesman had sold him the crampons without any straps! You'd think he would have suspected something at the shop, or would have looked in his pack during the three long days we were stuck in Liverpool Biv. Anyway, we tied the crampons to his boots and set off again.

Mike and Paul roped up and tested out the snow chute, but what was going to be a four-pitch belay turned effortlessly into a 32-pitch marathon, and there were still six of us to go and only one rope. Rather than wait for the doubtful return of the first rope we started to belay tentatively across a steep snow chute onto a rock rib, then back over into another chute. This was tedious, chilling work, and our confidence (or desperation) increased and we forgot about the rope and clawed up the exposed rock spurs anyhow.

The rock was sometimes firm, sometimes rotten, and there was constant danger of dislodging a boulder onto someone else. We were climbing the rocks with crampons on, and flailing away with our some-times essential, sometimes useless, ice-axes. We had enormous packs, with eight days of food and all the paraphernalia of a Christmas trip. We worked together, encouraging each other. Occasionally we ferried packs, and despite the cold, claggy weather, we were sweating with the effort and concentration.

I was the leader of this tramp and felt responsible and decidedly anxious as we hung around on crumbly rock ledges waiting for each man to come up. It was slow work, and the long wait in the bivouac had

The boys at the biv: (from left back) Ian MacLean, Mark Thomas, Paul Cook, Clinton Hayes, Mike Hollis; (front) Warren Thorburn, Dave Noble, Mark Pickering (1979).

not improved anyone's temper, but apart from a few muttered expletives our nerves held, and we gradually crawled up through the black rocks and suddenly reached the saddle just as the sun spontaneously burnt through the cloud. We still had all eight men, and by the time we got down to the Arawhata Rock Biv, we had clocked up a 13 hour day, caused by a combination of inadequate gear, poor route finding and inexperience in this sort of country. A friend told me later that he'd taken two hours to climb the saddle: we'd taken about eight hours from Liverpool Biv.

Yet it was profoundly satisfying, a hard day on tussock, rock and snow. We'd crossed not just the boundary of the saddle, but boundaries of our own competence and nerve. We'd been tested as we drifted from tramping into climbing, but pulled together as a team, and with patience and plenty of mutual encouragement, we had succeeded. With Arawhata Saddle bagged, the rest of the tramp was straightforward. Maybe we didn't have the collective experience to be in that sort of country, but ignorance can be a wonderful sort of bliss, and in the commodious rock biv that night, we gulped down the golden billy tea as if it were king's mead.

By the early 1980s I had decided that the printing industry was a dead dog, and I was now interested in pursuing my own gods.

I remember one day at morning tea in the composing room someone passed around brochures on the new 'film-setting' method. Most of the compositors were fairly scathing: 'It won't happen', 'just another newfangled idea', 'too expensive', and the universal assumption was that the hot-metal letterpress system would 'see me out'. I suppose by the early 1980s, barely five years after that brochure had been thrown in the rubbish bin, every apprentice and tradesman in that cosy little corner was either out of a job or had been retrained in film paste-up methods.

It's difficult to appreciate the speed of change. It was not some slight wind from the south, but a hurricane of new ideas and technology, a hurricane that has maintained its tempo with bewildering velocity. Hot metal and slugs went first, then in came machines with strange names like 'Phototron' and 'Fotoset', then they too got blown away by things called 'computers'. It's curious to recall that we were taught in printing history that the first linotypes of the 1890s were broken up by 'Luddite-like' gangs, who saw these new machines as a threat to their jobs. We laughed—well, we didn't even have *time* to form gangs to oppose the computer revolution.

I don't regret the changes. If I have nostalgia for my printing days, it is only sentimental tosh for an imagined past simplicity. In truth the old ways were filthy, crude, laborious and arguably dangerous. The lead dust that filled every cranny of a comp room did not do too many favours for one's health, neither did the endless use of solvents which we splashed around. Lead and ink would get so deeply ingrained into my hands that only after a two-week tramp would my fingers be ink free.

The changes in the printing industry made my skills virtually obsolete, and I spent two years on correspondence to gain University Entrance, and went into Victoria University in Wellington with not the faintest idea of what I was doing. Enrolment day was confusing, with stalls set up by the various departments genteelly hawking their wares. I put my name down for this and then that, then changed my mind and put down something else. Then I noticed a sign saying 'Religious Studies' and spontaneously signed up for 101.

It was an inspired choice. For 'Rels' is a mixture of philosophy and social studies, with more than a touch of anthropology, history and geography thrown in. It is a study of what people actually believe, as opposed to what they ought to believe (as in politics), or ideally believe (as in philosophy). It is the pursuit of meaning, which was exactly what I wanted to pursue.

In the first year I studied the general history and beliefs of religions, and in the second year, modern Christian philosophy under Lloyd Geering. This series of lectures subsequently became the basis for his book *Faith's New Age*, which I later read, but it wasn't as good as the real thing. The intimate setting of a seminar room, with only ten or so students, suited his style: low-key, discursive, exploratory. Sometimes I felt Geering was as engrossed upon the search as we were, and his depth of persuasion was compelling. After a lecture on Nietzsche we came out raving in favour of the Superman. After the Marx lecture we were communists. The Danish philosophy of Kierkegaard turned us into existentialists, and so it went on. The students discussed at length what Lloyd Geering himself believed, but it scarcely mattered for he carried us along into patterns of thought that most of us would not have believed we were capable of. In other words, he was inspiring.

Then I shifted to Canterbury University to continue my studies under Colin Brown. Actually I shifted to Canterbury for the Southern Alps, but I enjoyed Colin's tuition immensely, perhaps because of his old-fashioned courtesy and the fact that he had a stutter worse than mine. His third year course on Martin Luther only had two students, both of whom struggled to get to his room by the modest starting time of nine-thirty.

Hinduism at Canterbury University was taught by Jim Wilson, who used to be a climbing mate of Ed Hillary's and who had written a history of Mt Cook called *Aorangi*. Jim had a bushy grey beard and an inquiring chuckling disposition. His third year classes were on the Mahabharata and Ramayana epics, and also on Gandhi. Jim still had a mountaineer's rebelliousness in him, and no doubt in quiet defiance of academic logic and rules, used to tell us the questions he would ask in the upcoming exams. He did not see the rational justification for testing someone's knowledge merely on their ability to cope with surprises. Curiously, this made the exam harder.

It would be nice to recall that I was an exceptional student, but I was not. I was at best mediocre, motivated more by a personal quest for spiritual satisfaction than getting academic rewards. For eight years I crept slowly towards a Masters degree, but my study of the topography of the Southern Alps was brisk, rapid and first-class. Unfortunately, no degree course was ever offered in that subject.

The Godley is a vast valley, two kilometres across at its widest, and still nearly a kilometre in width at the top lakes. It is over 34 kilometres from Lake Tekapo to Godley Lake, and to walk up one side of the valley and back down the other is to walk for 70 kilometres or more, covering five of the old inch-to-the-mile maps. In summer the nor'wester can comb over the mountains and build a grey warm mass of storm clouds in the upper valley for days, while small ephemeral tornados whip dust into the air and then vanish into nothing.

But we did not have that problem, for we decided to walk up in winter. Just two of us, small patient dots in the company of white giants. It was a pointless journey. The valley was snow-plugged into a dead end, the passes shut for the winter. The air temperature was so cold that it hurt to breathe. Nothing grew along the sides, and the birds had shifted down to the benign climate of Lake Tekapo. We felt completely alone. This vast valley was ours.

For two days we plodded up one side of the valley, and then crossed the grey empty riverbed where the only trace of the mighty Godley River was a milky dust on the boulders. At Red Stag Hut there was one lonely pipit bobbing, and beyond that there seemed to be no life at all. Not even a kea called. The moraine was wearing pure white coverlets of snow, and the silence was intense.

At Godley Hut the temperature was minus six degrees inside the hut, and the glacial lakes were frozen by as much as 25 centimetres or more. As we walked across they screamed quietly, and every now and then we paused, just a little unsure if they really were solid or were setting a trap. We could peer right through the glass under our feet, and the sun glazed the lakes like icing on a cake, yet by two o'clock it was gone from the valley. We walked right up to the blue prism face of the Godley Glacier and gave it a friendly, ironic pat.

After a night in the hut we started to plod down the valley to home, which would take another two days. At Eade Memorial Hut (a place where hardly anyone goes) there was some turpentine scrub, which burnt and sparked in the tiny woodstove, a fire of life in the frozen desert. Cosy old shepherds' huts—Rankin Hut, Ribbonwood Hut, Sutherlands Hut—made us welcome on the way down, and since it was absolutely dark by six o'clock, we racked up ten hours of sleep night after night, as if our souls were ever hungry for rest.

But the Godley is not so inaccessible these days. Four-wheel-drive vehicles can get a good way up on both sides of the river, so it's silly to walk it. Wait for summer, hitch a ride when it's warm and the passes are open. Why make a five-day trudge for yourself?

But if tramping makes any sense at all, it is about enjoying the journey. Therefore walking up the Godley Valley in the middle of winter does serve a purpose. It's a way of living a deliberately slow life. A winter walk to nowhere, a meditation.

Starlight

Should be a-going, pull on my swag
Not much profit here to be had
I'll cash my cheque and drink my fill
Then join all me mates on the road
To the starlight hotel.

In this swaggers' chorus the starlight hotel is a roistering metaphor for sleeping without shelter under the stars. It is a lovely turn of phrase, suggesting that the wanderer enjoys the comforts of a unique sort of accommodation, rich in fresh air, natural beauty and an inspired sense of freedom. Only those individuals who have had the privilege of choosing their bed outdoors can fully appreciate the artistry that goes into the decision. My ideal spot would include: dry, yielding ground, proximity to a stream for fresh water, a fire crumbling into embers nearby and the long lingering reach of a tree branch that shelters you from the worst of the frost, yet allows you to see the stars glimmering through the slight shake of leaves in the wind.

You have to leave town to truly experience stars. Walk somewhere high on a moonless and star-dense night, and the entire hemisphere will seem full of creation. If you tramp really high into the mountains and camp by an isolated tarn, the surface of which is slowly crystallising with ice as the tussock stiffens with frost, then you get a strange sense that some stars are actually below you. If you start counting the stars, you will rapidly give up after the first hundred or so and acknowledge the magical assemblage as many millions upon millions of white light points, receding into the depths of unknowable space. In one sense you are completely wrong.

The human eye cannot see much below a sixth magnitude of light. Sirius, the brightest star in the constellation of Canis Major, is about first magnitude. Some people have counted the number of individual stars visible to the naked eye, and the answer is surprising—it's about 6000. I always find this rather a disappointing result, but it's actually necessary for our sanity.

If we could see every star in the universe then we would see no stars at all, just a blinding hemisphere of light, as bright as day. There would be no darkness, no visible moonrises, no inkling of dawn, no poetic sunsets. What saves us from this miserable fate is that the stars get in the way of each other and block each other's light. As well as stars there are gas and dust clouds that can create an apparent gap in space (one near the Southern Cross is called The Coalsack) like an open eye-hole through the fabric of the universe. The broad band of pale froth that we call the Milky Way is our galaxy, and it also creates a blockage of a kind, obscuring many other galaxies and nebulae.

It is not surprising that astronomical metaphors were often used by the men and women who lived and camped by the roadside: 'sundowners' were those who turned up for a meal in the evening; a 'moonlight flit' was the sly avoidance of paying a bill; 'born under a wandering star' meant constantly moving from place to place; 'the starlight hotel' and the coy 'sleeping with Venus tonight' were metaphors for sleeping out.

Incidentally, Venus is brighter than Sirius, and is often called the evening or morning star because of its visibility at those times, though sometimes it can also be seen at midday. The famous alpine guide Peter Graham remarked in his autobiography that he clearly saw Venus at noon as he was sluicing for gold in the deep, dark Callery River gorge. It has been stated, though I have never been able to confirm it, that Venus is only the third astronomical body besides the sun and moon to cast a shadow. You would need an exceptionally dark night with no moon, and a pale white surface to cast a shadow on, like a sandy beach or a dusty gravel road. One moonless autumn evening at 1200 metres altitude in central Otago, I thought I could detect the elusive Venus shadow against the pale grey shingle road, but that might have been simply wishing upon a star.

Night is never truly black, for there is always a backwash of light from the stars, and this 'lightness' at night can be rather a nuisance, especially when the moon makes a staged entrance. One fair evening we were camped at about 1500 metres just on top of Bald Mountain in the Olivine Range. It was late December, not long after the longest day, on a perfect windless South Westland evening. Warm and at our ease, we watched the last pink light as it caressed Mt Aspiring. Night did not seem to want to arrive, and at that altitude, even at ten o'clock, we could read easily. By eleven o'clock it was supposed to be dark, but the stars intensified their light until it almost felt like a pressure on our eyelids.

We could ignore the starlight, but we could not ignore the full moon. It rose at eleven-fifteen like a great orange saucer and started to beam down on us rather like one of those searchlights in old prisoner of war films. There was no escaping it. At two in the morning it was almost as bright as daylight as it probed through the flysheets and tents until we had to stuff our heads inside our sleeping bags to get away from its pitiless light. Finally we slipped into a fitful sleep as the moon sank very reluctantly at four-thirty; and then on the dot, at quarter to five, a glow in the east revealed that the busy old sun was eager to get us going again.

Should be a-going, pull on my swag...

Storm

About midnight a rustle of wind turns the corner of the hut and sniffs at the iron like a possum. There's a movement, a scrape of iron, then silence again.

Somehow the two sleepers in the hut sense that the weather is changing and shuffle over in their comfy dreams. The wind pulses and makes more sound, and the loose iron on the chimney bangs for the first time. The trees along the river bank make an anxious, irritated sound, as if slapping the air away unsuccessfully, and for the first time the mournful wind is louder than the creek.

Other loose parts of the hut start to whine as the gusts increase, and a few pits of rain sound on the roof. Within minutes the rain is steady, and the wind has increased strongly up the valley with big breaths, one of which is loud enough to bang open a window, which wakes one tramper up. He gets up, latches the window and peeks outside. Although there are a few stars to the east the cloud has swallowed the skyline, and he knows well enough that the weather has turned and a front is coming through. It's a bit late, but nothing will stop it now. He goes for a quick pee and as an afterthought grabs the dry kindling pile that they left outside last night and dumps it beside the dead fire. His mate hasn't twitched and the rain is getting steady.

By the time the tramper is getting ready for sleep the storm has woken his mate up. The wind and rain have gone from soft melody to heavy metal, banging away without much tune and shaking the trees with angry flurries. The noise increases on the roof, and both trampers are now awake but don't talk, for there's not much to say. They spend the rest of the night in a fitful doze as the full force of the front rips open the atmosphere above their heads and rattles their tin shelter with determined venom. The only consolation to the trampers is that the hut has probably withstood a thousand storms so far, and despite the singing wires and bashing iron, will see this one out all right. But it's hard on the nerves.

In the morning the land is sodden and the rain steady. There's no nice way onto the tops in this murk, and the little peaceful creek of yesterday has come up so violently in the last three hours that there's not a show of getting down the gorge either.

So this is where experience comes in. Back to the pit, slow the day's natural proceedings down until breakfast comes at ten, lunch at two, and you stretch the bladder till bursting before crawling out of the tangy comfort of your sleeping bag to dash outside. Someone might be keen enough to chop wood in the rain for a while. Someone else might forage around in the food cupboard and find enough old flour and butter to make a crude bread that smells divine and tastes like wood. Fire and billy tea, a few stories, the swap of chocolate, recollections of tramps long done, of people long gone back to a boring life. Studying the rafter poetry and making a few additions: a rhapsody for a rainy day. Making a biscuit last 20 minutes (it takes patience) and, most satisfying of all, planning for the next trip. Some of the best future tramps are plotted from the smelly bosom of a hut-bound day.

It's not a choice to be stuck there, but you make the best of it. Dozing all day, yet acutely sensitive to the wind noise, and waiting for the first detectable pause that is not the wind regathering its strength but running out of power. Perhaps about five or six, just as evening is sliding up the hillsides, the rain will stop. It will be quite sudden, and as the trampers peer outside they see streaks of pale blue between the grey clouds, and maybe later the moon. At midnight, the tramper with the weakest bladder will get up for a leak and step outside into pure still starlight.

The clouds have cleared, the wind gone a thousand miles away. The storm has passed by.

In many tramping club journals you will find the word 'Hughie' mentioned. Sometimes it's spelt 'Huey' or 'Hughey', but it essentially means the weather god. I have not seen the expression in hut logbooks dating from the early 1940s, and the first occurrence of the word I have found in New Zealand was in the *Tararua Tramper* from 1945.

The word, as with other tramping expressions, comes from Australia. *A Dictionary of Australian Colloquialisms* says that Hughie 'is the name given to the god in the outback, especially in the expression "Send 'er down, Hughie" used when it is raining hard'. It gives several uses of the word, the earliest from 1918 right through to a quote from the *Sydney Morning Herald* on a surfing contest in 1984 where an organiser said, 'I want to thank Hughie upstairs [Hughie's the surfies' name for God] for the waves [between 6 ft and 8 ft] and the good weather.'

How can an outback farmer's god that brings rain, also be a surfer's god that brings big waves? Another quote dates from 1946: 'Miners and prospectors would turn out and yell to a dull, dirty sky clouded with red dust, "Send her down! Send her down, Hughie!"' And from 1981: 'Incoming waves may be assessed, and sometimes the ancient cry will rise during a lull: "Send 'em up, Huey!"' One quote attributes the origin of the word to Charlton, Australia in 1905, but it might be considerably older than that, or even a corrupted aboriginal word.

No one seems quite sure whether Hughie is actually another word for God or an actual and separate weather god in his own right. I'm assuming Hughie is male of course. I don't believe in Hughie, but I can appreciate the chumminess of the name, as if you and a rain storm have an ongoing personal relationship, sometimes beneficial, sometimes hostile. It is hardly surprising that outback farmers, surfers and trampers have adopted a specific word dedicated to the weather, for it plays such a large part in their lives. Watching inches of rain an hour coming out of the thick, black heart of a West Coast storm is awesome and demands some sort of defiance and exuberance, a spiritual incantation from the godless lot—'Send her down, Hughie!'

If tested with the question, 'Where is the wettest place in New Zealand?', nine people out of ten would say Fiordland or Milford Sound. Milford Sound receives six metres of rain a year, so much rain in fact that at river outlets the surface of the sound is coated in a layer of one or two metres of clear, fresh water. You can swim in the sea without getting salty. In a nor'west rainstorm water pours off the granite walls of Milford Sound, and it is hard to believe that there could be wetter places anywhere else in the country—but there are. And the surprising thing is that these places are not in Fiordland at all, but further north, lying on the western side of the Southern Alps in a band of mountain areas from the southern glaciers of Fox and Franz Josef to the Whitcombe and Hokitika rivers.

For the record books, the aptly named Waterfall rain gauge in the Cropp River, a tributary of the Whitcombe River, holds the New Zealand record for the highest annual rainfall, recording 18,442 millimetres (18 metres) from 29 October 1997 to 29 October 1998. That's enough to submerge a four-storey building. Milford Sound settlement only gets a piddling six metres a year, though one rain gauge close to the sound recorded 13 metres in one year. The Waterfall rain gauge also holds the current record for the highest rainfall in 48 hours (1049 millimetres in December 1995) and in one calendar month (2927 millimetres, also in December 1995).

To put these figures in perspective, on average the annual wettest places in the world are in Mawsynram in India with 11,873 millimetres, mostly during the monsoon, and Mt Waialeale in Hawaii with 11,680 millimetres. Between 1860–1861 Cherrapunji in India recorded 26,461 millimetres (26 metres) in one exceptional year. It is by no means unlikely that the mean wettest place in New Zealand has yet to be determined, and by world standards New Zealand's rainfall is impressive, but if these figures seem astounding there is one more record to leave you in disbelief.

Passing a rainy day at Irthing Biv, Eyre Mountains.

Alex Knob is above Franz Josef Glacier in South Westland, a lowish, undistinguished peak of 1303 metres right on the fore-edge of the mountains, or what Coasters humourlessly call 'the foothills'. There is a good pack track winding up to the top of the hill, dating from the days when tourists were taken up for the views, which, should God grant you the right day, are truly spectacular.

It is a tramping aficionado's view. You look over Franz Josef Glacier into the deep gorge of the Callery River, and on to the Burster Range and beyond to the remote Tartare tops and the headwaters of the Whataroa River—places as difficult to reach on foot as anywhere in New Zealand. It's a view that is spoilt by even a scrap of coastal cloud, and there are perhaps only three or four days a year when the weather reaches such a peak of perfection and clarity that it's worth the long slog up to the top.

Most of the time it rains on Alex Knob, for it is positioned at the critical height where breaking westerly rainstorms are at their most intense. Rain-gorged clouds arrive from the Tasman Sea, cross the shoreline and within a mere 20 kilometres are forced violently upwards by the mountains, so that the first loads of rain are released in massive quantities.

In March 1982, after a dramatic storm in the Franz Josef settlement, a keen park ranger made a special and arduous slog up to the top of this hill to record the rainfall. He tipped out 181 centimetres, which was known to have accumulated in just three days (see *The Press* 18 March 1999). Now think about that: that's almost two metres, nearly three times Christchurch's annual rainfall—in just *three* days. If you had stood in one place you would have drowned.

Logbook Entry—Mudflats Hut, Arahura River, September 1991.
Arrived from Harman Hut yesterday, pouring with rain, so hut a welcome sight as very wet and cold—that's Goretex jackets for you—bloody hopeless.

Visitors to mountain country have a perverse relationship to bad weather. On the one hand it brings out a desire to challenge it: to cross swollen rivers and to negotiate high passes in mountain fog. But the other experience is to be humbled by the storm: to accept and enjoy a limitation of your abilities. By deliberately placing yourself in situations where natural forces can give you a difficult time, you are acknowledging your vulnerability.

Camping on the tops, where there is nothing between you and the gnawing wind except some thin, expensive nylon, is hopelessly optimistic. Tents, after all, are a compromise between lightness and strength.

No one particularly wants to spend all night hanging onto the tent to stop the thing exploding in fine shreds of nylon, but most of the time you get away with it. In one flapping, angry tent in South Westland, someone once sagely observed to me that in his experience most New Zealand storms rarely last more than a day and a night. Over the years I have witnessed the general truth of this observation, but as Charlie Douglas put it, 'The barometer doesn't affect the weather much on the coast', and the same cynical principle applies equally to the modern weather forecast.

In a multitude of logbooks throughout the mountains travellers have recorded their frustration and fear at a storm outside. Usually it's a case of waiting a day or so and then setting off again, exhilarated by the clearance. Here are a few examples of logbook entries from trampers who, after arriving at a hut on a fine day, have found themselves clasped to Hughie's bosom.

Haast Hut, Aoraki/Mount Cook National Park.
25-30 December 1965, G. Edwards, R. Mitchell, NZAC (slightly edited).
25 Arrived at sunset after long grind. Glass dropped suddenly during night.
26 Snow from nor'west, gusty winds.
27 Snow from nor'west, winds lessened.
28 The fact it was Mitchell's birthday did not alter Hughie's hostility. Low clouds, cold but calm in morning. Winds and snow increasing towards night. Down to last 3 matches.
29 Another happy day in the pit. Still snowing from nor'west. Hut has become almost buried in the last two days, except for the windswept doorstep. Shovelled snow off roof.
30 A break in the weather, but everything plastered. 8.45: retreated to Ball Hut. Another nor'wester looks to be on the way. That's climbing '65-'66.

This particular hut is halfway up the Haast Ridge on the way to the Grand Plateau in Aoraki/Mount Cook National Park. Before helicopter access became common, Haast Hut was on the main route to climb Ao-raki/Mt Cook, going via the Haast Ridge to Plateau Hut then onto the Linda Glacier to reach the summit rocks. These days it is rarely visited.

Waimakariri Falls Hut, Arthur's Pass
29 January 1977, Frank Gain and Roger McPherson.

Rain set in overnight with high winds. On 30/1 hut-bound in worsening gales with torrential rain and ferocious gusts. Midnight: had to batten the door against the gale. Stayed awake most of the night. 4 a.m.: electric storm with prolonged thunder and gusts of wind driving sheets of spray from the gorge uphill over the hut. Hut frequently shaking on foundations. Last lightning about 5 a.m. Gale continuing on and off. 31 January, morning: conditions moderated by 9 a.m., got some sleep between 6 and 10, but worsening again after midday. 1 p.m.: awaiting a lull to escape back to Carrington Hut.

Waimakariri Falls Hut is a small tin shed in an exposed alpine location on the way to Waimakariri Col. The hut is now about 40 or so years old, and the logbook is full of accounts from storm-bound parties. One party even strung a climbing rope over the roof in a somewhat desperate attempt to stabilise the hut.

McCoy Hut, Clyde River.
November 1986, Brian Deavoll, Pat Byrch and Bill Byrch. They were on an Arthur's Pass to Aoraki/Mt Cook traverse, and were waiting to cross the Francis Creek.

22 November: Arrived from Reischek Hut [Rakaia River] via Lyell Glacier and McCoy Col. Left Reischek late as intended camping on Lyell Glacier, but saw nor'wester brewing so decided to come on over. Glad we did as it's just started to rain! 11 hours. Day 7 AP-Mt Cook.

23 November: Raining, so moved nowhere. Rivers up.

24 November: Still raining, rivers up, but a few promising brighter spots, who knows? … that evening, blue sky beginning to show, but is that a southerly down valley?

25 November: It was a southerly. Snow down to scrub line, but still raining off and on, and rivers still not crossable yet ... Cabin fever setting in.
26 November: Above party leaving for St Winifreds Hut [Havelock River] via Disappointment Saddle or Fan Col. A horrible day!!!

McCoy Hut sits at the head of the Clyde River at the forks of Francis Creek and McCoy Stream, a beautiful and strategic site on the quickest route into the Garden of Eden, and also on the classic alpine traverse from Arthur's Pass to Aoraki/Mt Cook. But the hut can be trapped between two rising streams, and in the hut logbook from 1975 to 1998 there are many tales of woe, such as this one from December 1985:

It's raining again, oh no my loves at an end, it's raining again...

Here's my favourite from 15 January 1995:

Back again in detiro, deterioera, detereor.... worsening weather!

The Foster party in December 1985 waited for six nights, but probably the Auckland University Tramping Club broke the record with six consecutive besieged nights in March 1983 trying to get onto the Garden of Eden. When they finally had a go at reaching the ice plateau, they were promptly rebuffed and returned to McCoy Hut for another two nights. They then gave up and, disgusted with the climate, went out down the Clyde River to Erewhon Station. One member of that party was Penny Hazard.

Garden of Eden

What a difference it would have made if John Pascoe had not called this remote ice plateau the Garden of Eden. It is a name tinged with romance and irony, and it has become the focal point of some grand epics. He added other names such as Eve's Rib, Beelzebub Glacier and Eblis Gorge, and the adjacent ice plateau was named (I'm not sure by whom) the Garden of Allah and the passes daubed with names such as Angel Col and Satan's Saddle.

This account is by Penny Hazard, who was with a six-person Auckland University Tramping Club trip to the Garden of Eden in January 1982. The story is based partly on her account in the club's magazine *Footprints* (1982), but also on her diary, written at the rock biv shortly after the storm. It is a remarkable story of survival. They had reached the ice plateau from Hunters Flat Hut in the Wanganui Valley following a track on the true left of the Lambert Gorge, and were sidling around Mt Lambert heading towards Satan's Saddle and the Garden of Allah.

3 January 1982
Claggy and gusty, so pit-bashed until lunchtime, when the sun came out, with truly magnificent views. Beneath us was the Lambert névé [snowfield], and opposite us Mt Lambert itself. Further to the east were the Lambert Glacier and Mt Stoddart. The conditions were so favourable that we roped up and set off up the Lambert névé towards Satan's Saddle, fully expecting to get there in two hours.

Within 45 minutes the weather abruptly deteriorated and conditions became atrocious. It was impossible to make headway against the driving wind and snow, so it was decided to immediately construct a bivvy. It was already too dangerous to return over the crevassed névé in such conditions. The tent was erected on a large base cut out of the snow slope, and we snuggled into our sleeping bags, comparatively warm and cosy. The barometer reading had dropped to 750.

4–8 January

These days are hazy in everyone's minds. The snowstorm worsened considerably during the night of the 4th, with at least 1.5 metres of snow falling, burying the tent and most of the gear. In shifts, we would crawl outside and dig off snow, being belayed from inside the tent. Despite our best efforts we could not keep up with the enormous volume of snow falling down on us, the weight of which was also pushing us down the slope. By early morning on the 5th the situation was grim as the main tent collapsed under the weight of frozen snow and almost buried us.

We hurriedly abandoned this tent for the spare three-person tent and crammed six people in it. Most of our food, gear and packs were buried under snow, so there was no possibility of cooking food. The storm raged on unabated for 72 hours (three

Looking east along the Garden of Eden.

123

days) in a blurry haze of cramped conditions, howling wind and never-ending snowfall. We were continually clearing off snow to prevent a second burial. Our concentration was now on simple survival, and time was spent hugging each other, rocking and singing to keep warm.

By 7 January we were all suffering from various degrees of exposure, dehydration and exhaustion, and the strongest and the weakest party members kept swapping roles to boost morale. At times our behaviour became quite irrational, especially at night time, with feelings of disorientation, forgetting our names and sometimes collapsing. Our bodies ached immensely, even our jaws and teeth, and everyone was desperate for more sleep and more space, yet afraid that anyone who was allowed to doze might slip into unconsciousness. We all prayed for the wind and snow to stop.

Lack of air was a major problem, causing laboured breathing and drowsiness. We were using the tent like a large sack or bivvy bag with no room to rearrange ourselves. Additionally, the weight of snow was pushing or rolling the tent slowly downhill, so by now the exit was underneath us. In desperation a hole was ripped in the nylon for an air vent and people took turns to put their backs against the hole to stop the wind and snow coming into the tent.

In all, over the four days we were inside the three-person tent, we only consumed a handful of scroggin, and no more than half a cupful of fluid each, but we did not feel thirsty, nor desired to go to the toilet. Some people's hands had begun to ulcerate and my body was covered in a painful rash, that I was later told was caused by the rapid fat breakdown and release of fatty acids. Only by teamwork did we survive.

9 January

Beautiful fine day, what joy! We rehydrated ourselves by kneading snow in plastic bags and assessed our situation. We were all weak and quiet. My feet were very swollen and I could barely stand without support. By fossicking under the two metres of snow we began to retrieve our gear, and finding three more packs meant more food, more clothing and more chance of survival.

Our position was still very difficult. Avalanches thundered off Mt Lambert and blocks of ice and snow were falling all day on either side of our tent from the steep rocks above. Three planes passed overhead, but the violent flagging of an orange fly brought no response. First big meal today for four days, including Tararua biscuits and shrewsburys. By re-arranging and enlarging the tent we had our first real sleep—sheer bliss.

10 January

3rd day overdue by now, weather very still but a mist settled by noon. We had high hopes of a rescue helicopter and spent the day digging out the rest of the gear. People feeling stronger and walking better, and filling up with fluids. Urine still bright orange, and considered writing an SOS with it! Rationing food.

11 January

We felt certain by now that a search helicopter would have flown over the whole route if Search and Rescue had been alerted, but with continuing fine weather and no sign of the chopper, we suspected the truth [note: intentions and date out had been left with the New Zealand Forest Service in Harihari but were not acted upon]. Had to be positive, we were all stronger now, and roped up we retraced our route

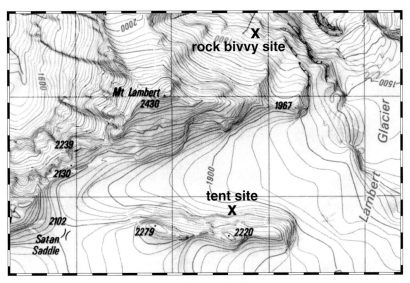

Site of tent bivvy and rock bovvy.

across the Lambert névé, and over the col onto the northern slopes of Mt Lambert. With numb feet, weak and tired, it was hard work, and we were worried about falling into crevasses which were now all hidden under fresh snow.

A note of our intentions and situation had been tied to an abandoned tent and it was decided that Matt and Sue should walk out, while the rest of us sheltered under a rock biv that we had seen on the way in, and Matt knew about from a previous trip. It was quite clear that we did not all have the strength, nor enough food for all six of us to walk out. As they left, there was an uneasy feeling of dependency, for we were relying on their getting out safely.

They retraced our original route and sidled back under Mt Lambert, following cairns we had made on the way in. Incredibly they reached Hunters Hut that night, and got out to the Wanganui River road end early the next day.

12 January

Another lovely day, with superb views from our rock biv. The four of us slept in to avoid breakfast, then there was one cracker for lunch, and we soaked dehy meat all day to halve the cooking time. Each meal was preceded by a drink of sweetened powdered milk. First decent wash for many days. Feet still sore.

13 January

Awoken by the sound of a chopper below us! Total white-out, and we listened excitedly as it hovered for ten minutes then gave up. It returned twice during the day but still could not land. Nevertheless we were overjoyed to know that they knew where we were, and far too excited and hungry to sleep. Sacrificed a lolly for a midnight feast, but still rationing food, as it might be white-out for days.

14 January

I started to read a novel which stated we should be grateful for everything, and so I adopted a different mental approach. 'Thank you God for an atrocious storm, for total white-out, no food etc ...' Perhaps it worked, since we were shortly awoken by the sound of two voices and I've never seen four people jump out of their sleeping bags so fast. These strangers, on being told they were beautiful, unleashed the food in their packs and we stuffed ourselves—one of us promptly vomiting it all back up.

Afternote: A trip that was supposed to last ten days, had lasted seventeen. We had been faced with a remarkable challenge, which only as a team did we meet. As the days and the nights of the storm passed, and the reserves of each person diminished, there was always someone there with enough strength to keep the others going. Only by looking after each other did we survive. The day it all ended, I knew I could head back to the mountains with the same party quite happily, and maybe even back to the Garden of Eden. I feel this is a reflection of the warmth and caring concern each of us had for one another. Never did anyone become selfish, as we all must wonder of ourselves, when faced with such a survival situation.

Seven days overdue and eleven days and nights since the storm first struck, they were all helicoptered out to Hokitika, suffering from varying degrees of frostbite. They spent several days recovering and reading their story in the newspapers. The members of the party were Sue Ensor, Kath Feeney, Chris Hardiman, Penny Hazard, Matt Johnson and Simon Leicester.

CHAPTER SIX

HUTS

U nlatching the door of a back-country hut at the end of the day is like a homecoming. The equipment and layout are familiar and calming. The routine of lighting the fire, warming the hut, cooking tea and having the last brew is profoundly comforting, and with the candle blown out and people settled into sleep and dreams, it is as if the hut itself makes an undertaking to look after its occupants patiently through the long mountain night.

There are over 1400 huts in the New Zealand mountains: comfy huts, cold huts, solid huts and huts that shake with every zephyr. Some

Huxley Forks Biv (1995).

have character stamped on each sheet of banged-together corrugated iron; some are large boring huts with signs stating 'no boots inside'. There are huts in the bush, on the tops, on river flats and by the sea. Some huts have been vandalised to extinction; others have been so fondly loved and carefully maintained by a shy deer stalker or a furtive tramper that you almost expect to find flowers in a vase when you enter.

There are huts that leak, huts that sweat, huts that smell of mutton fat, huts that fly away, huts that aren't on any map, and huts that are in the wrong place. You find huts that have burnt down and are sadly missed; and some that are like warts upon the landscape and you wish would burn down. But many huts sit so aptly on the land that you think they must have grown there, and these are cherished and may well record the persistent name of a solo visitor, popping in every now and again and chatting to the logbook, as if renewing an acquaintance with an old friend.

I confess to a deep affection for mountain huts. They are durable and vulnerable, a bit like the people who use them I suppose. A few get blown to oblivion but most hang on in there, and even with years of neglect they can still manage to do the job that they were set down on this earth for. They provide shelter, refuge, enjoyment, a meeting place for human contact and a crossroads for information and gossip. We replace our shopping malls faster than our mountain huts, which is probably why there are so few stories told about shopping malls.

This chapter traces the evolution of huts in the back country, from places of work and shelter for boundary keepers and deer-cullers to places of refuge and enjoyment for hunters and trampers.

Home on the Range

The headwaters of the great Rangitata River divide into three streams, the Havelock, the Lawrence and the Clyde, all lugubriously named after generals who fought in the Indian mutiny. An English gentleman, who was having a go at sheep farming at this remote confluence, rather fancied a classical name for his station and called it Mesopotamia, an allusion to the meeting place of the two great rivers the Euphrates and the Tigris. Just before the current Mesopotamia homestead, on the true right of the Rangitata, flows a broad shingly side-creek with the utterly inappropriate name of Forest Creek.

Even in Samuel Butler's day there was little beech forest in this barren valley, and there is less now. Just a skein of green skirts the sides while the rest of the landscape has yellow and white tussocks waving continuously to the skyline, occasionally riven with the crude grey gashes of eroded slips.

But what forest there was meant firewood, and there was water and some shelter from the nor'westers, so here Samuel Butler built his small 'V' hut, which should have been called an 'A' hut since it consisted of just a roof and little else. He later shifted to a cob cottage on the site of the main station, and Forest Creek became the boundary between Mt Peel Station and Mesopotamia. The owner of Mt Peel Station, J. B. A. Acland, built a boundary keeper's stone hut about a mile above Butler's old 'V' hut. It was built in about the mid-to-late 1860s, and may be the oldest surviving back-country hut in New Zealand.

We came to this hut in the winter of 1995. The hut was still useable, with four bunks and a fireplace that hardly kept the rooms warm. Firewood had to be collected from the beech forest across the river, which meant getting wet feet, and it must have been a numbing daily chore for the shepherds. There was something cosy, yet uncanny, about bedding down in such an historic building with a foot of June snow around the hut, a beech log fire burning on the grate and a severe frost crackling the air.

For a boundary keeper's hut it is palatial. There are two rooms with a huge stone dividing wall and an original colonial oven occupying the hearth. The thick exterior walls are made of greywacke river stones in two skins, with a loose rubble infill between—an unusual feature. But it is showing its age: graffiti is scrawled on every wall, there are some holes in the roof and a useful collection of old wire beds piled in a corner. The interior dried mud plaster is falling off in places, revealing the stone walls.

High-country runs in the 1860s had no fences, so shepherds had to be employed to prevent sheep straying across the boundaries. The work was isolated, hard and constant. The Forest Creek stone hut was lived in by a shepherd called Peter Keefe, of whom little is known except that he wanted land of his own, saved every penny and accordingly 'went about in rags'. The story goes that he lost all his savings in an unreliable trust fund and never recovered from the shock. This incident was fictionalised by David McLeod in a short story called 'The Stone Hut' in his book *Alone in a Mountain World*.

These traditional huts were once at the heart of the manifold operations of the high-country sheep stations, but four-wheel-drive vehicles have rendered many of the old huts superfluous. Apart from during the autumn muster, they seldom get used. The farmer hasn't the time to fix things up and the recreationist is usually not interested. Once the roof starts to deteriorate, it can mark the inevitable end of another piece of history, like the old boundary keeper's hut at Forest Creek.

Someone has recorded an original piece of poetry carved into the table in the stone hut, now owned by Ben McLeod Station:

Be wise my friend, eschew the crowd
And come up here to Ben McLeod
Don't drink too much, don't be a glutton
Breath mountain air and live on mutton.

We took photos in the brilliant air, restocked the hut with firewood and bolted the door in the forlorn hope that it would last a while longer. The hut is a lovely piece of history, about 135 years old, and listed as a Category 1 building by the Historic Places Trust. But history alone never saved a building; people have to care.

One of the most interesting old huts in the high country is Birdcage Hut in the Cass River valley, an anonymous tributary of the Godley River. The Cass is a dead straight, dull river, with a complete absence of forest or scrub along its valley sides. A more bleak place in the New Zealand back country is hard to imagine. It has hot, searing tempera-

General view of the Forest Creek stone hut in winter.

tures in summer and dry, crisp air in winter, when it gets deathly cold. On our winter trip in June 1987 the owner of Glenmore Station told us he had recorded a temperature of minus fourteen at the homestead near Lake Tekapo. We suspected that further up the valley, the temperatures we experienced were closer to minus eighteen. Even walking fast, clad in layers of long johns and down jackets, it was impossible to work up a sweat. The air seemed thin and exhausted.

Birdcage Hut is a basic musterers' design, one that has not changed much for a century and is repeated endlessly and creatively throughout the high country of the South Island. There are eight bunks for a standard team of men, including the packer, a large open fireplace and rather few home comforts, such as a table and seats. The internal framework is wood, with a skin of corrugated iron—no lining, but these huts were not intended to be used in winter, perish the thought.

Mustering gangs were usually six or eight men on the big stations. The undisputed boss was the head shepherd, and each shepherd would have four or five dogs, including header dogs who were silent and manoeuvred the sheep from the front, and huntaways who barked from the back and sides. The 'top shepherd' started early and went up to the tops to stop the sheep from escaping up hill. He might roll down 'German Doggies' or 'Irish Huntaways', loose rocks which started the sheep moving down.

Inside the hut, the 'packie'—usually the cook—was the boss. Cooking was not considered a skilful vocation: breakfast was mutton chops; lunch, cut mutton sandwiches; evening meal, mutton roast. The back legs of high-country sheep have all the meat on them, so the gang got those and the ribs for chops, while the dogs got the front legs. Potatoes and greens were available while they lasted, and maybe tinned fruit for pudding. Damper might be cooked on wet days, and if the muster was longer than a week the station would send up more bread and veggies.

Drying clothes could be an issue in crowded huts, and so could firewood. Even in the mid-1950s some gangs could still haul old totara logs out of river banks, otherwise patches of beech forest, ribbonwood and big old matagouri might have to serve. Many stations planted poplars and pines beside the mustering huts to supply a source of wood, and even today these tall signature trees still mark the presence of a hut or an old homestead that can be seen from a long way down the valley.

There usually weren't logbooks in musterers' huts, so the men improvised and wrote in pencil on the outside of the hut. At Birdcage Hut the pencilled entries are still as sharp and fresh as the day they were made. There's no smudging or fading, and despite the roly-poly surface you can trace the history of the mustering gangs of Godley Peak Station for almost 80 years. The oldest legible inscription is from 1898.

At the beginning of the twentieth century, the growth of tourism encouraged the building of a new type of mountain hut designed for enjoyment and recreation. At Aoraki/Mount Cook, two climbing huts—Ball Hut and Malte Brun Hut—were established in 1898. The latter had two rooms (a separate one for the ladies, of course) with four bunks, a wooden floor, and roof insulation of 'heavy felting'. Guides often carried a supply of wood from Ball Hut to supplement the kerosine stove, and the hut was protected from avalanches by a huge stone parapet. These were by no means the only tourist huts; there were huts at the Franz Josef and Fox Glaciers, some on the Milford Track, and the Waihohonu Hut in Tongariro National Park, which was built in 1901 and still stands.

The link between tourism and tramping was also important in the Tararua Ranges, with the Tourist Department granting £50 towards the cutting of a track to Mt Hector in 1910, and the same amount towards the building of a tourist hut on the Tauherenikau River in 1917. Alpha Hut had already been built in 1915 by the Greytown Mt Hector Track Committee, and it's hardly surprising that early interest in tramping in the Tararua Ranges was inexorably linked with the development of huts. Each year this range enjoys 80 clear days and 200 stormy days, while the remaining days on the tops are merely misty.

The Tararua Tramping Club, formed in 1919, was able to organise construction of its own hut on Judd Ridge in the Tararuas by 1924, built mostly by J. H. Gibbs and J. Fisk. Both men were experienced bushmen who had already cut the Marchant Ridge track in 1923. Their first job was to widen the track so that the supplies and iron for the hut could be brought up by pack-horses. Then the site was cleared of bush

Interior, Field Hut.

and the slope levelled. The timber for the hut was all felled from trees on site and sawn on the spot with a pit-saw. The weather was inevitably poor, yet the hut was completed after only five months work at a cost of £430.

Now 80 years old, Field Hut is New Zealand's oldest surviving purpose-built tramping club hut. I well remember the interminable night-time slogs up to 'Fields' on a Friday night. The hut was crowded, smoky and stuffy, and well before the last candle was out, the rats played among the high ledges that had been so thoughtfully provided for their enjoyment.

Gone are the days when my heart was young and gay,
Dim are the scenes of mud en route to Fields,
And Titahi Bay where I climbed so long ago,
No more do I go near those places—I'm too slow!
—Song of the Ancient Tramper

Field Hut's value lies in its cultural and social history and marks the flowering of a new tramping culture, particularly in the Tararua Ranges. From about 1910 through to the 1940s, many tracks and huts were established which in turn paved the way for classic tramping challenges like the Southern Crossing. This development influenced other tramping clubs around New Zealand, and reinforced the desirability of having dedicated recreational huts in the back country.

Other tramping clubs became busy with hut building, so much so that one keen Tararua tramper grumbled he spent more time on hut work-parties than actually tramping. Levin-Waiopehu Tramping Club built Waiopehu Hut in 1928 and Ohau Hut in 1930, though both had to be subsequently rebuilt after the huge storm of 1936. The Hutt Valley Tramping Club built Whare-iti Shelter in 1934, Powell Hut in 1939 and Waitewaewae in 1950.

The period of the 1920s and 1930s has been described as 'a golden era' of New Zealand tramping. It stimulated a good deal of exploration, track making and hut building, and did not seem unduly stunted by the Depression. It was, however, curtailed by the Second World War. Young men went off to fight, women went into factories, and there was little time to head for the hills. It was a great opportunity for the deer, and they seized it. What had been a problem before the war became a major environmental crisis after it, and precipitated the greatest hut-building boom the back country has seen or is ever likely to see again.

NZFS

For over 40 years the initials NZFS meant one thing to trampers: huts and tracks. But how so many useful facilities came to be built by the New Zealand Forest Service is a complicated story, and a backhanded tribute to the tenacity of red deer. The first Government deer culling operations began as early as 1922, and originally the NZFS controlled the business end. But in the 1930s responsibility shifted to the Department of Internal Affairs and Captain George 'Skipper' Yerex, who was one of the main architects of the extermination campaign. The main concern at the time seemed to be not the poor condition of the forest itself, but the threat to the stability of water catchments and the potential problems of erosion and flood run off.

Although high numbers of deer and goats were killed, the numbers left did not seem to be reducing sufficiently. After the Second World War, Yerex and his cullers resumed their military style battle (or as one wit put it 'Government farming'), but by the 1950s scientific research was revealing what many hunters and trampers already knew: that the existing culling strategy was not working, the mountain plants were taking a hammering, and there were more deer than ever. In 1956 the Noxious Animals Act was passed, and the NZFS got their old job back and got serious about it.

Actually, even with huts, tracks and a better understanding of deer behaviour, foot culling was never going to be the main instrument of destruction. That distinction fell to the inescapable helicopter. Ironically, as Chris Maclean pointed out in *Tararua*, the use of helicopters to fly in huts for hunters made it self-evident that hunting from the air was always going to be far more effective. Philip Holden in *Pack & Rifle* commented:

> *The remarkable thing about helicopter shooting, when it did start on those blocks I had hunted [as a government culler], was just how many deer they brought out. It certainly put paid to the popular notion that government hunters were eliminating the deer. The reality was that on most hunting blocks government parties were more or less holding the deer population at what can be termed a manageable level, though at times they were unable to keep up with the annual birthrate. Red deer are nothing if not resilient.*

Simple, unadorned and no longer orange, Pine Valley Hut in the Richmond Range (1996).

Over 600 huts and bivouacs were built in the mountain ranges for government deer cullers between the late 1950s and late 1970s. Their placement was generous in the extreme, and any mountain range that needed them got them. Hut building was particularly intensive in some of the North Island ranges, including 40 or so in Te Urewera National Park, 30 in Kaweka Forest Park, a staggering 50 or more in the Ruahine Range and 20 in the Tararuas. Local tramping clubs even complained that the wilderness experience was being jeopardised by all this unnecessary civilisation.

As a rule of thumb, the huts and bivvies were spaced at about three to four hours walking distance, assuming fast tramping by a culler with a light pack, dog and gun. The idea was that the culler could shoot freely while travelling between huts without being burdened by a heavy pack. Huts usually contained all the necessities, including blankets, food, axe, billies, camp oven etc. Since there were relatively few other users in the hills in those days, there was no need to lock the food cupboards.

Down in the South Island, the number of huts built is quite mind-boggling, and these are general estimates only. The Richmond Range got 30 or so, North-west Nelson (now Kahurangi National Park) got 20, Nelson Lakes 10, Lewis Pass 20, and so it goes on. Almost all the big east coast valleys, like the Wilberforce, Matthias, Hunter and Dobson, got a few huts in them, but some of the heaviest concentrations came to be in the West Coast valleys, like the Toaroha, Kokatahi, Whitcombe/Hokitika and Waitaha. There were perhaps at least 50 huts built on the West Coast alone, but that figure may be conservative.

The hut structure was usually a timber frame with flat metal sides, a corrugated iron roof, large open fireplace, table, food cupboard, four or six bunks built onto the wall, woodbox in the porch, louvre windows, and not much else. A water-tank might be added for a dry tops hut, with the guttering directing rainwater into the tank. The standardised loo was always 30 metres away. The NZFS also had standard designs for upright two-bunk bivvies and the infamous 'dog kennel' bivvies. They were all painted orange.

Have these huts been bettered? Probably not, and it would be nice to know who came up with the famous design. According to Arnold Heine (*FMC Bulletin* April 2003), Max Cone was the senior civil engineer at the NZFS headquarters in the 1950s who was responsible for the hut programme, and may have been the designer of the six-bunk hut. There is a hut blueprint with his initials from 1958. (Ron Weatherhead was the mechanical engineer who came up with the design for

Duchess Stream Biv, Lewis Pass (1992).

the equally robust and versatile suspension swing-bridge.) The original huts used Dexion, a sort of large boys' meccano set, and interestingly there is at least one example of such a hut on the Waihao River called, inevitably, Meccano Hut. But the sheet-metal walls proved too cold, and wooden framing and lining became the norm.

The Department of Conservation has subsequently spent a good deal of money on designing bigger and better huts, but for some elusive reason, rarely manages to capture the spirit of the simple NZFS huts. They are basic, practical units, well suited to the men who had to live in them for months. There was nothing flash or clever about them, but they kept dry through wet spring storms, were airy in summer and warm through winter. They did not intrude on the landscape, and were often positioned superbly well by men who knew the value of being close to water, firewood and views.

The bunks were ranged around the central focus of the fireplace or woodstove, which made the evenings convivial, efficient and welcoming. For a solo culler (and many of them were) they were comfy, but at a squeeze you could fit eight or ten people in. In the four-bunk Park Peaks Hut in the Ruahines on one very wet club tramp in the 70s, we fitted thirteen inside: eight double-bunking, four on the floor and one up on the 'luggage rack' above the door. I doubt if this is a record.

In the later part of the twentieth century, the mountain areas saw a rapid decline of working people in the hills. Rabbits were being poisoned from the air, and deer cullers had been superseded by helicopter killing and recovery. It was then that the value of these mountain huts began to be appreciated from a recreational point of view. It's not so absurd to say that one of the reasons that tramping became so popular in the 1960s and 1970s is the huge legacy of NZFS huts and tracks. They quite literally opened up the back country.

The first time I saw Kiwi Mouth Hut was in January 1979. It was a dot of orange on the dry brown river flat as we came sweating down the hot Back Ridge track, our knees rattling down the hard rocky surface. The kanuka was brittle with heat, and it felt as if the whole of the New Zealand summer was pouring down onto this one wee hut in the Kaweka Ranges. Opening the door was like opening an oven to a blast of warm air, and a swarm of blowflies came buzzing out. We stripped off and plunged into the deep pools of the Ngauroro River, and by the time we were dry the hut had cooled down enough to ship our gear in.

We lit a fire, though it must have been 35 degrees outside, but Heather McKean had spotted some flour and had a fancy to make a loaf. Funnily enough, the draught from the fire seemed to clear the air from the hut, but Dennis Hole and I stayed outside in the shade, sipped tea and idly watched Heather scouring the camp oven. I glanced over the map and realised that Kiwi Mouth Hut sits at the heart of a matrix of routes.

By my reckoning you could tramp in six different directions: down the Ngauroro River to Kuripapango, or up the Ngauroro to Rocks Ahead Hut. There's the ridge and tops track to Mansons Hut, or a slog up the opposite ridge to the old Kaweka Hut. Back Ridge is a bone-dry route (like every ridge route in the Kawekas) onto the biv and further still onto the hut, or, if you fancied a moister trip, you could try Kiwi Stream itself. This leads onto another track to Kaweka Hut or right up to the obscure Studholme Saddle Hut and the high point of the range, Kaweka J itself. All good choices, on good river routes or tracks, and few huts in the back country give you that sort of choice.

My loaf of bread (1979).

Kiwi Mouth was a meeting place, the junction for gossip and hard-luck stories for many of the early deer cullers of the Kawekas. There would always be someone at Kiwi Mouth, or something interesting in the logbook. If it was a hot summer you could dive into the deep pools of the Ngauroro; if it was cold, you could burn kanuka logs on the open fire and yarn through the night. There were trout in the river and a deer or two in the bush, and it was far enough away from any road end (a good five to six hours in any direction) that only the few remaining good keen blokes made it there.

Well, I must have been a good keen bloke in those days, for one month later I was back at the hut on another week-long trip in the Kawekas. My tramping mates were Chris Hutchings and Ross Gilmore, and it was my turn to make the loaf of bread. Six months later I was back again, on another six-day circuit with Nick Miller, Jan Simmons and Mark Thomas, but this time we only slipped through.

The last time I went to Kiwi Mouth Hut was in November 1982 when I was on my own. It was a rare Kaweka day because it rained. I had tramped up the Ngauroro River and arrived at dusk—a soft, soothing time in these barren hills. The firewood box was full, and I wasted little time in getting a fire roaring, and in the late evening leafed through the logbook, taking pleasure in reading my own name scrawled over that full year of 1979. The manuka smelt sweet, and the Ngauroro River sang loudly in the night.

I packed up in the morning, heading for Mansons and Otutu huts. I latched the door and shut the louvres to keep the blowflies out, then crossed the river, and when I looked down from the ridge after an hour's hot hard work, I could still see a tiny orange dot on the river terrace. It's been 22 years since that day, and of course I'd like to go back, but how often have I said that?

A Prevalence of Huts

It was a really dark and stormy night when I finally got to Flora Hut, bedraggled and somewhat peeved after a long, wet slog up the hill road. My car would not take the steep, slippery grade, so I was reduced to old-fashioned methods to get up to the hut. The welcoming open fire was as good a cliche as I wanted, filling the hut with warmth and light. A man and his son were having tea, so I joined them, and after the young boy had gone to bed and was slumbering happily, the man suddenly started to talk about his separation from his wife.

It came out in stuttered, frustrated phrases, and I had no choice but to nurse my cooling cup of tea and listen. Apparently he'd been left to care for his son after she'd taken off with another man. Of course I only got his version of events, but he stated emphatically that I was the first person he'd really talked to about the separation. It was because I was a stranger he said; I was coming into the hills and they were heading out, so we would never meet again. His words burnt a lot more hotly than the fire for a while, so I was relieved when both he and the fire calmed down to embers and we could let the matter rest.

In the morning the goodbyes were brusque, almost shy, but this is the interesting point. On three separate occasions I have been in huts with men and their sons, all strangers to me, and heard three different and bitter stories about separation and divorce. Could these conversations have happened anywhere else but in a mountain hut?

At a fair calculation there are about 1400 huts in the foothills and mountains of New Zealand at the moment, and about 1000 of these belong to the Department of Conservation. I have visited 910 huts so far and wherever possible taken a photo for the archives. There are some tramping club huts, though not as many as there were, and other odds and sods, like the scheelite miners' huts in Glenorchy, or research huts that have been eerily abandoned, like Camp Creek underneath Mt Alexandra on the West Coast. About 250 to 280 huts are owned by stations, mostly in the South Island high country, and are generally little used, except by the birds.

At the old station hut up the Dobson Valley, Nic Bishop and I were awoken one morning by a sharp volley of gull song from the outside porch. Unable to see the bird we were somewhat incredulous, a black-billed gull in a hut? Then suddenly a magpie warbled away, followed by the unmistakeable screech of a kea! Was there a bloody aviary out there? Next, incongruously, into the swaddled air of the hut came a more-pork's hooting, as if an owl was perched on the rafters with us.

By this time we were beginning to suspect this avian Pavarotti, but rather than disturb the performance we kept very quiet and listened. Over the next 20 minutes we detected bits of pukeko, fantail, blackbird and bellbird, so who was the exceptional vocalist that achieved this range? A starling.

For the amateur hut statistician in New Zealand there are several surprises. For instance, the highest hut in the country is not in the South Island, but beside the Crater Lake of Mt Ruapehu. But Dome Shelter at 2670 metres does not really count, especially as you can't even stretch out your legs, so the title properly goes to Empress Hut in Aoraki/Mount Cook National Park at 2500 metres. Pioneer Hut on the Fox Glacier névé misses out by a whisker at 2350 metres, but gains a certain notoriety by being the most shifted, renovated, redone, rebuilt and redesigned hut in the country. I am not certain how many Pioneer Huts there have been, or if anyone has kept count, but I think it is five (or six) (or seven).

The biggest hut in New Zealand is currently the 80-person Pinnacles Hut in the Coromandel Range, and the smallest would be any number of one- or two-person 'dog kennel' bivouacs. Currently DoC is building large numbers of cloned 10-bunk huts, with practical insulated walls, useful vented windows and shiny stainless steel benches. I should not complain, and I guess the possums won't notice the lack of character, which reminds me ...

Winter photo of Dome Shelter, Mt Ruapehu (about 1981).

One winter we arrived at Hodder Hut, which sits at almost 1500 metres, virtually under the shadow of Tapuae-o-Uenuku, the high peak of the Kaikoura mountains. There's nothing green up there, just rock and snow. But that evening one member of our party heard something outside and discovered a possum ekeing out a miserable existence near the hut. 'I did it a favour and put it out of its misery,' he remarked as he described how he ran around outside the hut flailing at the possum with the hut axe.

Then he skinned it, gutted it, chopped the resulting carcass into bite-sized pieces and fried it up on the roaring primus. We admitted it was very tasty, and after we'd satisfactorily consumed all the edible parts of the animal he quietly told us the beast had been living in the toilet.

I remember that possums were also a nuisance at another hut. We had arrived jubilantly at Rocks Ahead Hut in the Kaweka Range, drenched from a day's tramping in the rain. But our expectations of a warm, snug hut were dashed when we found it squatted in by the local possumer, who had hundreds of possum skins drying from the rafters, making us duck apprehensively as we entered. The stench was awful, and the black-bearded possumer had a rather creepy, fossicky manner about him ('Like a possum himself,' muttered my mate under his breath), and he was wearing a wide-brimmed sun-hat, which puzzled us.

'Oh well, you see, it's them,' the possumer said, pointing up at the steaming skins. 'They got maggots and they drops out all over the place, and I don't like 'em in me hair.'

One-nil to the possumer. We camped outside.

The oldest logbook I ever came across was at Eric Biv on Agony Island in the Havelock River. The first entry was in 1948, with John Pascoe's name as an early entry in 1950.

February 26–March 10
John Pascoe, Bernie McGlynn, S. Conway.
Swagged up Havelock River, but ice at foot of Outram rock ridge too hard to cave-make, unfortunately we had no brace and bit, nor explosives. So we had to swag up the Havelock icefall to 6300 ft (20 minutes from Disappointment Saddle). Cold wind and north west derision [sic] on the main range. It took six hours of solid work to make a cave, which was into hard névé snow. The hut's long-handled shovel was very awkward to use and much of the work had to be done by a man lying on his back hacking and scraping with an ice-axe while the chips went into his pipe or down his neck. We both got wet thru and very cold. We called it a cave by 7 pm, laid flat rocks on the floor and unrolled the underfelt, then settled in.

Two days later they were back to the relative comfort of Eric Biv, where they had persistently grotty weather for ten days or so—there is a lengthier account in Pascoe's book *Land Uplifted High*.

Eric Biv is situated on an isolated moraine island called Agony Island in the middle of the upper Rangitata River, and was built in 1948 for £6 by the Canterbury Mountaineering Club, which is still currently maintaining it. Timber was carried up on pack horses, and they planted poplar and lawsonia trees on the island for firewood. Agony Island was so named, I've been told, because of its sandflies. One entry in the logbook stated firmly:

> *Please don't touch Neil Hamilton's stores: four men are relying on them being here in mid-winter 1953. Thanks.*

Then someone had crossed out the 53 and pencilled in 54?, then 55?, then 56?, and apparently Neil Hamilton never did get to those stores, for they were still there in 62?.

Incidentally, the odd collection of trees around Agony Island seems to be due to A. S. D. Evans, who in August 1953 revealed that over three days he had planted larch, macrocarpa, ponderosa, douglas fir, acacia and sycamore, amongst others, as well as a gooseberry bush '10 yards' from the hut. On a flat 800 metres above Veil Creek, near a patch of 'dead boring ribbonwood', he continued his planting zealotry with the same introduced species. Then, to finish off, he scattered seeds of cedar, monkey puzzle and juniper around the island, noting hopefully that the juniper berries might produce gin.

Talking of planting exotic trees, a strange tree had been planted next to the Kowhai Hut in the Seaward Kaikoura Range, resulting in this interesting exchange of views in the logbook (May 2002):

> *Ranger Dude! I don't think planting a willow next to the hut is a good idea, firewood or no firewood. They spread rapidly along riverbanks. Keep it clean, keep it natural!*

This elucidated the following comment:

It's an apple tree you tosser.

It's rare these days to find hut logbooks more than 30 years old, and the Department of Conservation whips away half-filled logbooks with a bureaucratic diligence that I regret. There was a 30-year-old logbook at Studholme Saddle Hut in the Kaweka Range, and another, rather unexpectedly I thought, at Castle Rock Hut in Abel Tasman National Park. South Opuha Biv has its original logbook from 1975, which is barely half full—not surprisingly perhaps, since every single imperial, metric and CD-ROM map has the hut marked five kilometres from where it actually is.

The most ill-fated hut in the mountains must surely be Three Johns Hut on Barron Saddle in Aoraki/Mount Cook National Park. It was built in 1959 by the Canterbury Mountaineering Club as a memorial to three climbers who died in 1955 attempting to climb Mt Cook. They were John Hammond and John Young, both from England, and an Australian, John Vidulich. It is a notoriously windy site, as this quote from the logbook suggests:

20 January 1962, Auckland University Tramping Club
Nor'wester blowing at full force; the walls are moving in and out like a concertina, the sudden changes in pressure causing our ears to pop continually. We don't have to go outside to collect water—we just park a pan under the broken window. At the time of the most violent gusts we belayed people outside. Often we get a short silence, and then before the next gust hits the hut, we can hear it roaring across the divide for several seconds—then we shake, rattle and roll again.

At some time on 30 January 1977 a tremendous gust broke the re-straining wires and blew the hut off its foundations over the saddle and into the head of the Dobson River. Four young mountaineers were in the hut—Craig Benge (25), 'Bill' Bennett (19), Fenella Druce (25) and Robert McLean (19). There were no survivors and the bodies were not recovered for several days (see *The Press* 3–9 February 1977). Subsequent donations by the Druce family and others enabled a new hut to be built at the head of the Cobb River, called simply Fenella Hut, and a replacement hut was built on Barron Saddle.

The loneliest hut? In the North Island there are not many huts that you cannot reach in one (albeit long) day's tramp from a road end, but in the heart of the Kaimanawa–Kaweka massif there are a few that must take a day and half to get to—Boyd Lodge, Te Puke (Ohikarua) Hut, Harkness Hut and the lonely bush hut in the dense solitude of the Mangatainoka Valley.

But my favourite is Otutu Hut, two good days from anywhere. It sits at 1280 metres, just on the edge of the beech forest with a view over the widening tussock tops of the Kaimanawa Ranges. It was built for the deer-cullers in the 1960s, and I can see why. When I arrived there one evening I made a brew, and because I had run out of candles, watched in gathering darkness and incredulity as five red deer came out of the forest and grazed just a few yards from the hut door.

In the South Island the most isolated huts are in Fiordland—the Landing Stage at Puysegur Point or Deas Cove in Thompson Sound. To reach Puysegur Point would take four days of hard tramping, and another four to return—a thoroughly good waste of a week, but hardly anyone goes there on foot. In a sense, huts like Deas Cove are not really remote, for they're visited regularly by float planes ferrying fishermen, their tackle and their booze.

However, there's a difference between a hut being geographically remote, and a hut that's rarely visited. In 1991 we stopped at Island Hut in the Eyre Mountains, and if we believe the logbook, which we did, then no one else had been there for three years! On the West Coast of the South Island in 1981, when we arrived at County Hut on a tributary of the Waitaha River, we found the last visitor had been there exactly a year earlier—a not unusual occurrence. Curiously, someone later told me that they had visited County Hut nine months later and our names were still the last ones in the logbook.

Mungo Hut, Sir Robert Hut, Price Basin Hut, Tuke Hut—there must be 20 or more huts on the West Coast that only get three or four parties a year, and may even go a year or two without seeing anybody. So it is important to bolt that door behind you and make sure every window is closed! One possum can pretty well stuff a hut.

Actually, a hut does not have to be really isolated in order to *feel* isolated. Such huts don't get too many visitors of course, but those that do visit look after the place. An isolated hut always has a full wood-box because of the character of the people who visit; perhaps they spend the day chopping firewood in simple satisfaction at being there.

Huts like Griffin Creek on the West Coast come to mind, or the Alfred Hut in the Clarence Reserve, or Stafford River below Jacksons Bay. When you arrive the billies are clean and upside down, the mattresses aired, and at least two stools are placed by the beckoning fireplace which, in a perfect world, does not smoke. There are plenty of candles to burn and a fine set of billy hooks waiting to be employed. When you look around you notice that little repairs have been made by modest visitors, who obviously care about the place. The wood fire crackles and flashes off the dark walls as a deepening day slips to sleep. Your companion starts to snore, a fingernail moon slips over the black beech canopy, and a kiwi makes its first breakfast shriek into the night.

I was able to visit so many huts in the mountains because for years I was a State-employed tramper. I was paid a decent wage (called a bursary) for five years to be a university student, and with care it was enough to live on. Then there were always PEP and student employment schemes through the summer months, and the dole plugged any gaps. Every other keen male tramper I knew was doing much the same, and we hitch-hiked up and down the Southern Alps with long hair, scruffy beards and a marvellous sense of irresponsibility.

But I also had a job, not, to be honest, proper paid employment, but an extra justification for my bohemian lifestyle. I was writing a book, *75 Great Tramps*, which started as an idea in a hut in 1979 and was finally published in 1986. It was the first general guidebook to tramps throughout New Zealand, though there had been specific guidebooks, such as Philip Temple's track series and Nick Jennings' *Tararua* guidebook, and it turned out to be popular enough to warrant a reprint, and then a revised edition which was expanded to *101 Great Tramps*.

I had no training as a writer; I learnt by making mistakes and some of them were awful. Still, the readership proved forgiving for in all the years of being in print I received only two letters of complaint (quite justified) about my instructions in *101 Great Tramps*, and one fan letter. One book led to another, and in 1988 I wrote a book on tramping

Evening at Waterfall Hut, from left: Dale Parsons, Kirsty Woods, Rex Benbrook. (Other member of party Anita Catchpole).

called *The Hills*, then another guidebook, and before I had time to realise it, I was making a living and the government was rid of me at last.

All back-country users are voluntary, hard-working members of the hut appreciation society—each one of us has given consideration to what makes a great hut, and it's not as simple as it sounds. You cannot compare a tops hut, with guaranteed views, to a bush valley hut; a hut on the bush edge is a completely different beast to an open valley hut, but all have merits of location. Then you have to include factors such as the size of the hut, whether it has an open fire or a woodstove, bunks or sleeping platforms. Finally there are the intangibles—the character of the place, its history, whether it welcomes or repels. The following shortlist commends some huts, which stand out in part because they were visited on memorable trips with great companions.

For my pick, one of the best bush valley huts is Waterfall Hut in the Ruahine Range. It sits on a low beech forest terrace at the confluence of Waterfall Stream and the Kawhatau River, and what makes it special is its sense of isolation. It is in the heart of the Ruahines at the junction of many possible routes. Trampers who get there in a weekend will have had a hard day in, and face an equally hard day out.

It's a classic six-bunker, as basic as it gets, and it has an air of satisfaction and serenity. It's witnessed many summers of trampers passing through and hunters arriving for the autumn roar. It is a hut that you would like to linger at, but invariably you've run out of time or the rivers are coming up, and you bolt the door with a pang. You promise yourself that next time you'll bring more grub and stay a week.

Down south there is an abundance of open valley huts that occupy the immense emptiness of great east coast valleys, like the Rakaia and the Wilberforce, with a certain defiance. Many huts are nestled into pockets of beech forest, partly for access to firewood, but also to escape the howling nor'westerlies that funnel down the valley and stir up ephemeral dust tornadoes. It is an experience just to tramp up one of these yawning gaps in the mountains, where tall peaks stab abruptly into the distance over riverbeds of unending, unyielding gravel.

Whole valleys are full of attractive huts, like the Dobson River, for instance, or the Hunter River, or the awesome Godley River—just take your pick. But my favourite is Unknown Hut; it's off a branch of the Wilberforce River and sits in the middle of a huge tussock terrace dotted with large clumps of hebes, which from a distance look like green

Unknown Hut, Sven Brabyn outside and Tom Halliburton in the doorway.

Moeraki boulders. Even the midwinter sun reaches Unknown Hut early, and from the doorstep you look up to the massive spiky southeast face of Mt Murchison.

The hut is, again, a standard six-bunker (I have a weakness for standard six-bunkers) with an open fire, and because it squats at the broad junction of several valleys there seem to be unlimited opportunities for exploring almost anywhere. Moa Stream, Unknown Stream, Burnett Stream to the Avoca River, Gibson Stream to the Mungo Pass, or the Wilberforce valley on to Browning Pass are all options. It is a hut that gives a sense of where you may go the next day, or a good feeling about where you have been. And it has such an evocative name.

A bush-edge hut should stand exactly on the margin of the bush and the tops. It's no good being buried 100 metres or so down a bush spur, you want to see tussock almost at the hut door and a fine view from the small window. It should have altitude and attitude, and be a place to gather strength for the foray out into the tops, or a refuge to be grateful for after a hard day over the range. Howletts Hut in the Ruahines would do, for it is a classic bush-edge hut, and I'd happily add Otutu Hut in the Kaweka Range or Ellis Hut in Kahurangi National Park to the list, but I have chosen differently.

Scamper Torrent Hut on the West Coast is more scrub edge than bush edge, but as you slog up the steep spur from the Waitaha River, you get a dramatic sense of arrival thanks to the impressive views of the rugged tops up to Mt Durward. There's a kero stove, no sandflies, four bunks and a logbook full of complaints about the steepness of the bloody hill. Some entries emphatically state that the writers are never going there again, but they will. Or they will want to.

A genuine tops hut has to be 'out there', exposed, and require some sort of struggle over a hill to reach its battered tin walls. It shouldn't be too easy to get to and, ideally, should be able to be glimpsed from some way off, making it both alluring and frustrating. When you arrive it should be tidy and homely, with small personal touches from a few previous visitors. The logbook should be a good read, with people you know the names of doing interesting trips. And the quality of reading material should be unusually high, making it easy to stretch out the sleeping bag and bury yourself as the storm lashes the outside. The hut should shake a little in the wind and the wires should hum.

Strangely enough, true tops huts are quite rare. Adelaide Tarn in Kahurangi National Park, or Ivory Lake at the head of the Waitaha River come to mind. The old Forest Service nearly always kept their huts near supplies of wood and water, which meant building huts on the bush edge.

Mangahuka Hut in the Tararua Range does fit the bill. It is surrounded by tussocks and sits beside a rare tarn. Cut off by the Tararua Peaks on one side and the deep valleys of the Otaki and Waiohine rivers on the other, the hut seems psychologically rather unbalanced on the ridge, and the immense satisfaction of arriving there is muted by the consideration that it is a bloody long way to get out.

Break-In

You would not normally expect an epic in the Orongorongo mountains. They are too close to Wellington; a quiet-mannered little range, where the highest peak does not even protrude above the bushline, and the idea of doing a serious tramp there would strike people as funny. Most Wellingtonians call them the Rimutakas, but the main river has the rather melodious name of Orongorongo. It is a mild waterway, and four-wheel-drive vehicles can go up and down its wide shingle flats easily. There are over 30 private cabins and huts lining both sides of the river, though if you walked up it you would hardly know they were there, apart from a peek of roof, or the odd glint of a tin chimney caught in the sun.

My idea was to go up to South Saddle and on to Mt Matthews, the high peak, then down to the coast at Ocean Beach in Palliser Bay. I think I was going to walk back around the coast, or hitch-hike or something, but it doesn't matter because I never quite made it that far. I had left my run fairly late and it was already evening by the time I got to South Saddle, where I made a fly camp. The southerly must have hit about midnight. It was a boomer.

The wind ripped the guy ropes out of the ground, and the fly flapped liked demented washing, and by the time I got myself sorted out and re-tied the guy ropes my sleeping bag was soaking wet from the hammering of the rain. It poured down all night, and then got cold. Just on morning, after a miserable wet night, it seemed to clear up. After some deliberation I took advantage of the clearance and headed on up to Mt Matthews. By the time I got to the summit, the southerly started to make me think again, and then it got really personal. Hard, cold rain set in, and the summit, if it was the summit, was a damp squelchy bog of saturated bush, moss and lichen.

I hurried back to South Saddle and down to the Orongorongo, but I was out of luck. By the time I got to the river it was raging: a brown, ugly mass of water that seemed to be clawing wider as I watched. With not too many choices left, I put up the fly and slopped into my sodden sleeping bag. I had on all my clothes, including bush shirt and long johns, but by about midday I was shivering uncontrollably.

It was numbingly wet and cold, and I was *inside* my sleeping bag. Mountain Safety Council literature had earnestly drummed into me

Tree stump in storm, on the way up to South Saddle (1989).

157

that shivering was a warning sign of hypothermia, and I was well beyond the early stages. Another half hour or so and I'd probably fall contentedly asleep and die of hypothermia in my sleeping bag, a ludicrous but very real proposition. The Orongorongo River was seething and a foot higher since I'd put the fly up, and Wellington city might as well be on the moon for all my chances of getting there. How was I to get warm?

Then I remembered the baches, and recollected there had been a side-trail not far from the start of the Mt Matthews track. With a big effort I pulled on my boots, stuffed the useless pit into my pack, abandoned the fly, and thrashed down the true left of the river, sometimes wading through surging eddies of dirty water. I found the track and followed it to a bach, which was locked. I rattled the door helplessly and eagerly peered through the window at the fireplace and large stack of dry wood beckoning beside it.

It wasn't a hard decision. I was still shivering with the physical effort of getting there, but before bashing the front door down I had a quick squiz round the back and there was a small miracle. A busted pane of glass had been temporarily blocked up by a piece of plywood. I hauled myself onto the window ledge and with one hard kick broke open the plywood and was through the gap and onto the floor of the bedroom. I was still so cold and befuddled that I attempted to crawl back through the hole to get my pack, without realising that I could now release the catch and simply open the front door.

It took a painful 20 minutes to start a fire. My own matches were soaked, and I scattered many of the hut's matches with my shaking hands. Finally, the paper caught and the kindling crackled. I piled on log after log, but only after three brews of tea in my stomach and some two hours in front of the fire did I start to feel genuinely warm again.

The Orongorongo River reached its peak about three that afternoon, a swirling evil body of brown water carrying black logs down to the sea. The din was tremendous. At four o'clock it suddenly got colder and stopped raining, and by six there was faint sun. I had spent all afternoon by the fire, the sleeping bag on my lap, patiently spreading out the wet down with my fingers and counting interminable blessings, for all the world like a monk measuring his beads in a cell.

I didn't sleep well, and had to get up once and stir the embers to make another hot drink. Once you get profoundly cold it takes ages for the body to recuperate, yet by degrees I drifted off to sleep. At daylight the world was a different place; the sky was perfectly clear and the river had dropped drastically. I went back and untangled my fly from several pieces of driftwood and an inch or so of mud that covered the campsite, then cautiously crossed the river at midday and headed for home down the Seven Mile track.

Before I left the bach I carefully restocked it with firewood and re-placed the plywood over the missing window, but I have often wondered whose place it was that saved my bacon. I cannot remember if the hut had a name, but the dunny was unusual. I remember it to this day: an old red telephone booth. I'm sure the owner will recognise it now, so, belatedly (about 20 years late), thanks mate. I owe you one.

CHAPTER SEVEN

SOLO

I n the *New Zealand Geographic* magazine of 1989 there was an article written by Michael Abbott about his solo traverse of the Southern Alps from Fiordland to Golden Bay. Abbott claimed he was the first to do this great journey, some 1600 kilometres all told—an impressive achievement. His article, however, subsequently generated a letter from another man, Rex Hendry, who modestly pointed out that he had completed a similar solo traverse in 1983-84, as part of an overall tramp from Cape Reinga to Doughboy Bay in Stewart Island.

An old homily painted inside the first Powell Hut, Tararua Ranges, which I'm sure a few ancient trampers will remember: 'There are three ways to attain wisdom: Meditation, the noblest; Imitation, the easiest; Experience, the bitterest.'

In a curious aside, Hendry mentioned that while he was undertaking his traverse, he met two other people attempting similar journeys. Over many years I have seen other logbook entries from men and women on the same mission—Swiss, German, American—sometimes in pairs, but often alone, for how would you persuade someone else to accompany you the entire length of the South Island?

These solo marches are impressive, but they immediately reminded me of perhaps the greatest solo tramp ever undertaken in New Zealand. In 1836–37 a warrior chief called Te Puoho, along with 40 warriors and women, tramped from Golden Bay down the entire length of the West Coast, and over the Haast Pass to Southland, a distance of some 1500 kilometres. It was an ambitious, bold and foolhardy raid to attack a Southland Maori tribe, which ended in death for Te Puoho and enslavement for the rest of the party—with one exception.

A Maori warrior named Ngawhakawawa, Te Puoho's brother-in-law, managed to slip away from the clutches of the Southland Maori, and retrace the terrible journey back to Golden Bay. Alone, living off the land for food, crossing the great South Westland rivers and pared down to the bare resources of his strength and determination—surely this is one of the greatest solo treks recorded in European or Maori history.

People have always undertaken solo journeys, whether by choice or necessity, and like other trampers I have pushed my luck and gone on solo tramping trips. Did I enjoy myself? Yes, by and large.

Solo tramping is often a sign of both maturity and desperation: maturity because there are some special qualities needed to get out in the hills on your own, and desperation because the reason is sometimes just a case of not being able to find anyone to go tramping with. Perhaps solo tramping starts as desperation and then becomes addictive—there is a deep satisfaction in managing for yourself. I'm sure tramping on my own gave me the time to enjoy thinking.

A Voice in the Mountains

We left Marks Flat early one morning and descended down the rough Saddle Creek onto Monro Flat. We then climbed out of the Clarke River valley, up McCullaugh Creek and over an unnamed bluffy pass to the head of the Paringa River. It is a lovely, lonely place. On one side were the ice-fields of Mt McCullaugh, a 2266 metre peak, and on the other was the awesome buttress of Douglas Spur. It was February 1985, and the day was windless and rather ominous under a grey blanket of South Westland cloud. We had not seen anyone for a week, so it was startling to hear someone call out.

The four of us stopped in our tracks and looked about, seeing nobody. Then came a second shout which echoed about the narrow valley. We saw a single figure picking its way out of the cloud and the sky, and moving hurriedly down the rocks off Mt McCullaugh. When he got down to us he seemed really pleased, 'Haven't seen anyone for days.'

It was Murray Watson. I knew him quite well from the Canterbury University Tramping Club, and I was as surprised as he at the unlikely meeting spot, for you don't expect to bump into people in the heart of the South Westland wilderness. We chatted away—he had just climbed Mt McCullaugh and was keen to know details of the route over to the Clarke River. The others wanted to move on to the rock biv round the corner, and we invited him to join us there for the night, but he seemed edgy and motivated. He thought if he pushed it he could get down to the Clarke River that evening, and with a quick goodbye we drifted off on our own separate ways.

Later that evening we camped by the Paringa rock biv, which sits in an eyrie-like position high above the Paringa River. The clouds cleared and the full majesty of the mountains around us was revealed. It was massive country, emblazoned with the late fire of sunset, and it was mighty hard country to go solo tramping in. Around the camp-fire we chatted about Murray and his motivations. We didn't think he was mad, indeed in many ways we admired his courage at tackling this sort of country on his own, but we all agreed on one thing—he was pushing his luck.

It would only take one slip on a steep slope or one river crossing that was too deep to put him in jeopardy. Even coming up McCullaugh Creek that morning we had been grovelling over huge slimy moraine boulders in the bush, and some of our scrambles had taken us more

Looking up the head of
Paringa River to the saddle.

than five metres above the ground—easily enough height to slip on the wet moss, fall and break an ankle. What chance would you have in such a place if no one came to look for you? Even if someone did come, would they ever find you? You could lie for days, with no water, waiting for rescuers who, in all likelihood, would never arrive.

Murray did manage to reach the Clarke River and in the end came out down the Landsborough, though how he got across that huge river on his own beggars belief. He died somewhere else in the same year though, crossing into the County River from Ivory Lake. His last entry in Ivory Lake Hut logbook stated enthusiastically that 'the weather was too good to waste'. His body was never found.

Solo tramping offers experiences that are unavailable to the person who always has a companion—a closeness to nature, for example, perhaps because you travel more quietly and your presence in the bush is so slight. I have walked up to and almost touched a red deer that was feeding on the track, quite oblivious to my presence. Birds come closer to the lone tramper and seem less afraid. Your senses are uncluttered and acute, and you hear night sounds from the bush that you never seem to hear above the chatter of a tramping party.

One evening near Okarito in 1982 I listened for half an hour to the beautiful calling of a bird that I simply could not identify. Well I could, because it sounded like the kokako I had heard in Pureora Forest, but South Island kokako were supposed to be extinct. At the very end of the haunting call, in the last few seconds, it changed sound slightly and resembled a tui. Subsequently I have read that tui may imitate kokako calls if they are in the vicinity, but whether this was a real kokako or a tui imitating one I cannot say. What I can say is that these experiences often seem to happen when you are alone.

People travel more safely in groups and always have done. Weighing up choices with other people invariably leads to safer decisions, even though the party may be less experienced. There are clear objective dangers in tramping on your own, river crossing being the obvious example, but there are also more subtle dangers that can cause solo trampers to occasionally disappear off the map.

When tramping on your own your assessment of risk is impaired—you have to make every route decision and every choice. Because you are more vulnerable in the mountains it might be expected that you would make conservative, safe decisions, but in my experience that isn't neces-

High Burn, a side valley of the Hunter River.

sarily the case. Your motivation is higher and that seems to put stress on your decision making. You have set a goal and are more determined to make it to the top or get to the other side. In a mutual decision, a group of trampers might decide not to risk a river crossing, and because the decision is shared the sense of failure is lessened. Solo trampers are perhaps more impelled to take a chance because the sense of failure is not shared—it's theirs alone.

It's a peculiar psychology. They say 'he who travels furthest travels alone' and I can understand that now. There is a deeper drive at work, for trying to conquer yourself and your own fears makes you personally

165

competitive and weakens your judgement. By and large you get away with it, but on the way you get a few frights.

In 1986 I was tramping alone, and left Blue Lake Hut in Nelson Lakes National Park intending to head over the Waiau Pass. It was an ambitious trip for the time of year—a wintry May with fresh snowfall on the slopes above Lake Constance. As I skirted high above the lake I stepped into a snow gully that instantly became a hydroslide. The snow was so powdery and light that my ice-axe just slopped around in air, and for several seconds I was whisked down the slope at a great velocity until brought up sharp and hard against a rock jammed in the snow gully. It knocked the wind out of me, and I was left half dangling over a small bluff, some four metres above a ledge, which in turn was above another ten-metre bluff into the lake.

I got up, dusted myself off and carried on. The slide was over so quickly I hadn't had time to be afraid, and yet after some minutes I began to feel queasy and unsteady on my feet. The day had turned forbidding and grey, and realising that perhaps I wasn't in such a good condition to continue over the pass, I retreated back to Blue Lake Hut. By the time I got there one leg was stiff and bruised from the fall. I boiled the billy, sat down and started to shiver. Mild shock had set in, I suppose, as it dawned on me that I had been very close to disappearing off the map myself.

Nerves

I was on my own walking up the Cass River, a wide, uninteresting braided river-bed on the route to Cass Saddle, which then follows two bush valleys around to Lagoon Saddle. The Cass–Lagoon, as it's known, is a popular tramp near Arthur's Pass National Park in Canterbury. It suits easy-to-medium level trampers, and indeed is popular with first-timers. I had tramped the Cass–Lagoon several times, with clubs, in private groups, with a girlfriend or two, and twice on my own. I knew the route backwards and frontwards, and had camped in half a dozen spots on the way. So it was all the more inexplicable that I should dump my pack down on the dry river-bed and say inwardly, 'I can't go on.'

For some minutes I had been feeling a profound sense of uneasiness, even fear, with a compelling desire to turn back. I could not pinpoint the logic of it. I was tramping in a safe, easy valley, the weather was fine, and this was, after all, what I most enjoyed doing. Yet I could not shake off a complete sense of helplessness, even futility. Inner voices were saying, 'You are tired of this, why continue when there is no pleasure in it any more,' and just at that point of time the inner voice was exactly right. I chucked my pack down and sat staring doggedly at the majestic view, trying to recapture what it was in the landscape that had, only half an hour before, appeared to give me so much pleasure. The mountains were grey piles of scree, the river bed was a desert of stones.

They call it 'losing one's nerve'. It is a loss of confidence, embarrassingly sudden, and not necessarily in places that are steep or extreme. All the enjoyment you felt in your pursuit drains away, until you are left with a sort of pointlessness. It might last for seconds, and no one sees it; or it might last for years and be regarded as an illness. I've seen it happen to people on middling to nothing slopes, and now it was happening to me, despite the fact that I knew perfectly well that I had the skills and competence to continue with the job, and had been in far harder places before.

Of course, these feeling don't just arise in trampers. In every walk of life people have moments of intense doubt and then manage to carry on. The 'crisis' passes, your nerve is regained and you carry on, keeping the 'failure', if that's what it was, to yourself. Men particularly treat these moments as secret failings, rarely, if ever, speaking of them. Maybe they feel that to reveal weak links in their personal armour is to make themselves too vulnerable, and perhaps there is some strange evolutionary purpose in not confiding these thoughts to other people. Or perhaps it is simply that confidence is everything in our society: if you have it, you have everything; if you don't, you have nothing.

Needless to say I said nothing about these feelings to anyone. Then, quite unexpectedly, a friend started to discuss a strangely unnerving weekend he had had on his boat, and suddenly I realised that his experience exactly mirrored my own. He was an experienced sailor, had been to Fiji and back and sailed around the North Island, so he was hardly out of his depth on Lyttelton Harbour. Yet he described the weekend as one of entire uneasiness. On the boat with his mate he was constantly worried, anxious about the wind and their anchorage, and hardly slept at all. There were several minor gear failures, which in themselves were nothing much, but somehow they rattled him, causing an inexplicable loss of confidence. There was nothing he could put his finger on. He had not been on the boat much at the time and had approached the weekend with pleasure, expecting to enjoy himself, so it was all the more inexplicable that the opposite had happened.

Over the years I have tried to analyse why these losses of confidence occur in people, but the more I think about it the more inscrutable it seems to be. Human beings have a dynamic personality range and our confidence levels fluctuate. We are not always in equilibrium and we have to work at maintaining it. It is almost as if we have a bank of confidence inside us, which we have actively nurtured and increased since we were children; but then gradually, as we go through adult life, we take it for granted and use it wastefully. Unless we keep adding to the bank, the amount of confidence inside us slowly erodes without us noticing, and sometimes when we make a sudden personal demand we realise that there's nothing there.

Buckland Peaks, Paparoa Range.

Yet why do these doubts strike at the very root of the things we most enjoy? It would be understandable to be nervous about making a public speech when you have had little practice, or about facing the challenges of a new job, but why lose faith in the things you do so well? I suspect what I've observed in myself must happen to everyone, that there are doctors who lose confidence in treating their patients, mothers who get panicky handling their children, company directors who lose faith in their business judgements. Maybe some folk never lose their nerve, or perhaps they are better at hiding it. We keep going because it is the only alternative

In the old days you would have been told to 'get a grip on yourself'. Self-reassurance does seem to work, but it can be a difficult trick. If, however, we accept that a range of physical illnesses forms a normal part of the human condition, then surely the mind is allowed its range of illnesses, from lapses of confidence to the blues to full-blown depression. But there is a more comforting way to look at the matter: would we expect normal human beings never to have doubts about themselves or their abilities?

For the record, on that sunny Cass river bed I scoffed down some chocolate and persuaded myself to carry on a bit further to Cass Saddle and, by slow degrees, teased myself gently out of the despondency. By the middle of the day I was romping along the bush track, savouring the mountain smells and wondering what the hell all that had been about. I still don't know. As my friend remarked, journeys into the mind are the most interesting journeys of all.

Patupaiarehe

It was a hot summer trip on my own in the Hawdon Valley in Arthur's Pass National Park. The Hawdon is not an interesting valley—dusty shingle mostly—but on the river's edge are terraces with some good grass campsites amongst the beech forest. I was feeling knackered after a long day coming over Tarn Col and found a cosy little grass clearing, just downstream from a much larger one. I put up the tent, started a fire, and as the late afternoon sun dipped behind the Polar Range, I drank a brew of tea and felt well satisfied with the day's effort.

By eight o'clock the stars were sharp and I snuck into the pit, identifying most of the night sounds and ignoring those I couldn't. The river got louder as the night deepened, and a half-moon illuminated the beech trees with a faint silver. There was a slight down-valley wind, but it was peaceful as I dozed off, and I sleepily congratulated myself for picking such a quiet spot.

Then wouldn't you know it, I heard voices. Not far away either. I peered from under the tent and saw some torches flashing through the big clearing some 50 metres away, and heard an occasional shout. Bloody hell, so much for peace and quiet. I drifted off again, then heard some bursts of singing and looking out saw a flicker of firelight. There must have been three or four trampers, noisy ones too, and obviously completely unaware of my presence. I was really awake now, and half in annoyance, thought I might as well join them and have a chat. I shoved on my boots, grabbed a torch and pushed past the skein of pole beech between the two flats.

'That's odd,' I thought, 'where are they?' I could see most of the large grass flat in the moonlight and it was quite empty. Where could the fire have been?

Perhaps they were behind those trees, or those ones? I scouted along the edge of the flat, then crossed it one way and went back the other, becoming more and more confused. There was nobody—no fires, no voices, no singing, no people. A morepork suddenly screeched nearby and my torch jumped from tree to tree. Was it really possible that I had imagined the entire thing?

I searched for an hour for the phantom trampers and slowly became convinced that the whole episode lay within my imagination. In a half-sleepy state I had clearly strung together a few strange rustles and some insistent music from the river, added a few twists of wind and a bit of dancing moonlight, and conjured up out of thin air a whole insubstantial pageant of trampers, fire, voices and songs. I could even identify a couple of their tunes. I went back to bed thinking of the line from

Shakespeare: 'We are such stuff as dreams are made on.'

Then I remembered the patupaiarehe, the name Maori give to the spirits that inhabit the misty mountain tops or deep forest at night. Were they real, or a poetic way of explaining the suggestive sounds of a forest at night?

This phenomenon of being alone in the bush at night has been expressed rather well by Arthur Dudley Dobson in a passage taken from his autobiography *Reminiscences*. In the 1860s he was walking on the old Takaka pack track from Golden Bay to Motueka, and bedded down for the night somewhere near the summit, perhaps under a limestone overhang (of which there are several). There were no stream sounds to block out the other night noises, and it is interesting that he usually attributes a particular sound to a particular cause.

I gathered an armful of dry fern and made a comfortable bed. Here I lay down and listened to the voices of the night and forest. The kiwis called to each other, the kakapo followed; they seemed to hold quite long conversations. The ruru, owls, held a conference, which was interrupted occasionally by loud screaming, which echoed through the mountains like the cries of a maniac, and was very alarming to anyone hearing them for the first time. The slightest movement of trees caused creaking and groaning, and with a vivid imagination one could hear conversations being maintained all round, the sounds resembling questions and answers. Insects of all kinds were making weird noises, the cicadas would set up a shrill trill, and the wetas made a loud creaking sound, as they called to each other from time to time. Conversations innumerable were carried on everywhere. Loud cracks came from the trees every now and then as the expanding growth cracked the bark; then for a time silence was only broken by the slight movement of the leaves, a sound unlike any other, a soft murmur, not like the sounds made by the wind, but a very slight sound, as if caused by the light falling on the leaves. These sounds came just at dawn.

The Ghost of Whariwharangi Bay

Whariwharangi Bay lies at the far north of Abel Tasman National Park, a beautiful stretch of golden sand backed by old rustling macrocarpas and rapidly regrowing manuka forest. It's a lonely place now, mostly visited by trampers who stay in the old homestead which has been turned into a proper tramping hut. In 1978 when I visited, it was still virtually untouched: an old two-storey wooden building with two rooms on the ground floor and a couple of rooms up top. There was a big open fire in the downstairs room that looked much the same as when the farmer and his family walked away. There was still wallpaper on the walls.

'Why worry' Bay must have broken their hearts after years spent clearing the bush, and trying to get enough grass growth for the stock, always aware of the isolation—it was a two-day tramp to the nearest store or doctor, or even a bit of company. The homestead is a short distance from the sea, situated in a sheltered glade, and the day I arrived it was warm and drowsy with bees buzzing and the air heavy with nostalgia. I tried to imagine the family's faces as the evening drew in.

I was sure there was no one else in the bay—several times I thought I heard voices, but it was probably just the murmuring sea. I drank generous amounts of billy tea, sleepily swallowed a meagre meal and turned in early. It must have got dark about eight o'clock; I heard a morepork's call and was half asleep when I heard two deliberate steps on the ceiling.

I sat up. At first I thought I had imagined it, but no, there they were again … two more steps, quite firm, coming from the upstairs room above my head.

That was the room with the closed door, which I had not bothered to look into. I held my breath and waited, my heart starting a faster rhythm. There was a long heavy pause, and I began to feel I was hallucinating the whole thing when there were three or four more steps. Solid real steps; not those of mice, rats or possums, I was sure. It was chilling; they sounded just like human steps, but I thought surely I was the only one there.

Perhaps someone had been asleep upstairs all that time. If so they had been bloody quiet. I hadn't been, chucking down firewood, singing a tune—were they that shy? I heard four more slow steps. It was the deliberateness that made the hairs stand up on my neck, as if there was a person up there who was also trying to be deathly quiet, trying not to wake me. What was he doing up there? I got out of bed, switched on the torch and crept out into the hallway. I shone the light up the stairs and the beam fell on the closed door. There were steps again, furtively creeping.

I did not like it at all, but I could not just hang around the hallway all night while this bloke crept about the upper storey. It gave me the willies, and anyway what if it wasn't a real person at all? I opened the front door and looked outside—nothing but moonlight. Slowly I walked up the stairs, testing each step, trying not to make them creak. Why didn't I shout out, 'Hey, you, anyone up there?' I seemed to be infected with a sense of secrecy, or menace. Actually, I was scared that a total silence would fall and I'd be worse off than before.

I reached the top of the stairs and slowly turned the handle. There didn't seem to be any light from under the door. With a last grip on my courage I tightened my fingers on the handle, swung the door abruptly open, and swept my torch inside the room. Empty! I was beginning to deflate with relief when there was a sudden rush of steps and a flutter of feathers as something darted out of the room straight between my legs, and thumped down the stairs and straight out of the open front door into the moonlight.

Bloody weka!

CHAPTER EIGHT

BREATHING EASY

W e must meet thousands of people in our lifetime. We begin with our family, then move through many school chums and later teenage groups. Then add up all the workmates in all the differing jobs; the numerous social acquaintances in clubs, pubs and weekend sports; flatmates too, a hundred of them probably; perfect strangers travelling on buses and trains into exotic lands, together mangling some sort of communication out of the bits and pieces of languages; our partners in life, and the ones before, which we continue to carry inside us; our children and their children. And so it goes on, personal encounters of every persuasion—but how many people do we really get to know?

Conversation in the upper Makarora Valley: Jonathan Jull, Kirsty Woods, Rob Delamore.

People are the stuff and staff of life, the breath that gives impetus to our lives, yet we communicate spasmodically. It's just the human way: we are busy with our own lives and our own sweet selves, so we are short on time and short on listening skills. But imagine a scenario where a group of friends are gathered in a place that has no distractions: no television, or telephone interruptions; no rush to get to work or rush to get away from it; no traffic to negotiate or family crises to sort out, or things needing to be urgently fixed; no stereos blaring from next door, or bogans revving their engines out on the street—in fact hardly any sound at all, except for the rush of a river or wind through the trees. People might pay a fortune to create such an opportunity and escape from stress, yet it happens every time you go tramping.

It is astonishing how much time you have on your hands once you leave all the business of daily life behind. Walk up any river valley, and you will find an undisturbed place to camp; all you have to do is bung up the tent, start a fire and cook tea. During that time you have an entire evening at your disposal for social interaction—conversation, joking, teasing, arguing, mulling, thinking and telling stories. Isn't this what life is about, or have I missed something?

The Red Hills

This week-long tramp in the Red Hills was packed with incident, and seemed to me to have all the ingredients that make trampers' journeys so satisfying—wild landscapes, the adventure of new country, unexpected encounters and the sharing of these experiences with friends whose company you enjoy.

In late August 1993 three of us—Sven Brabyn, Dave Glenny and I—loaded up my Hillman Hunter station wagon and headed over Arthur's Pass to Haast and the Red Hills. There was a snowstorm forecast for the pass, and I didn't have any chains, so we hoped to sneak through. However, as usual, the frontal cloud proved faster than my Hillman (nicknamed 'Mel' because the colour on the registration form was 'caramel') and we reached the pass after dark with snow blurring the windscreen.

Determined not to waste a minute we chugged on through the village and reached the original Bealey bridge, which I'm sure some people will remember. It was a single-lane job with a very awkward approach and a steep climb out of it. You couldn't get any sort of speed up on the bridge because there's a snappy little corner just before the climb, and it forced Mel into first gear, as the tyres just couldn't grip on the ice and light snow on the road. Some brave revving did not improve matters, and we slid gracefully back to the bridge, blocking it for everyone else. The only hope was to reverse, and with the others pushing I got Mel into an obliging mood and managed to graunch and slither back uphill towards the village.

We were contemplating a grim winter's night sleeping three-up in the back of the wagon when I remembered Rob Delamore, a friend of mine, had a bach in Arthur's Pass. I rang him from the store and he was happy to let us use it, so we got the key from the store lady and in an hour's time were sitting beside a roaring log burner with hot coffee, complaining that the Red Hills were not getting any closer.

Though Sven pestered me to buy chains I resolved to wait till the snow melted, so by ten o'clock we were back on the road to Haast and the Cascade River, which we reached with no more fuss at about six in the evening. Dave, the botanist, was chuffed because he found a rare daisy he was looking for beside the roadside verge. I was pleased because it felt great to be in South Westland again.

Crossing the Cascade turned out to be manageable, and we gradually picked our way up this mighty river, our large packs wobbling on our backs. We were heading for the saddle over to the Gorge River, which is at the northern end of the Red Hills, and somewhere about Kappa Creek, as we were bush bashing upwards, we stumbled across a piece of history forgotten in the bush.

It was the original Cascade–Pyke Valley Road, built in the 1880s and marked 'overgrown' on my 1975 map. We could follow it quite easily, despite the trees growing out of it, and it appeared to be going our way. It seemed a somewhat surreal convenience in the wilderness of South Westland, and when we arrived at a clear area, with a trickle of water down a smoothish rock face, we thought what a perfect spot to camp it was. I knew from my historical research that Charlie Douglas had helped build this 'road', so we put up our tent, made a brew and said, 'Thanks, Charlie,' while watching the smoke from our fire mingle with the twilight mists gathering in the valley below.

The next day we lost the pack track on the saddle and it took us most of the morning to bash up onto the Red Hills proper, a pretty parkland of tarns and beech forest spoiled by a drizzling mist. We camped early by a tarn, and the beginning of the third day was spent navigating along the range in a thick peasouper. We sat down for lunch near Telescope Hill pondering the mist and wondering just how high above our heads it really was, when a rip of blue followed by another gash suddenly exposed the strange rolling plateau of red rock. It was a superb surprise.

These ultramafic rocks are rich in asbestos and other minerals in which plants struggle to grow, and the tarns looked like blue-green opals in what could have been a barren red landscape borrowed from the Australian outback. At sunset the colours of the red rocks deepen to an extraordinary ochre, and indeed it was Joseph Banks on Captain Cook's *Endeavour*, in March 1770, who first pointed them out: 'A mouldering soft stone the colour of brick or light red ochre.'

Sven and I had a lazy lunch while Dave ran off eagerly collecting daisies from the rocks. But, after an hour of views, the cloud started to creep back over the hills again so we were off, over Telescope Hill and down a bush spur, with some hard bush bashing to the Pyke River. The final push of a long day was along the old bulldozer trail (made by the Kennecott mining company in 1973 to get to the Red Hills) to the hut at Big Bay.

We were stuffed and the hut was full of whitebaiters with buckets of slimy treasure. I can't recall if we got any whitebait patties or not; I think they begrudgingly gave us a small portion as an apology for taking over the hut. Anyway we slept in the lobby, as the nor'wester started to blow ominously.

It was hosing down by the time we got to the Gorge Burn Hut the next day. After slogging over beach boulders that Charlie Douglas had aptly called '12 pound cannonballs' we were glad to find the hut empty and dry. It had been a long day from Big Bay, just mountains and sea and a bitter rain pounding on our backs—it felt as if we were on the edge of the known world.

We settled in, then paid a courtesy visit next door to Robert Long, 'Beansprout' as he was known, his wife Katherine and their two shy children. They had lived at the wild and remote Gorge River off and on for five years, with just the company of trampers and cray fishermen or deer stalkers who dropped into the airstrip. But they were by no means out of touch with the rest of the world, for they had good reception from National Radio, and Beansprout reckoned his kids had spent more time in helicopters than cars.

With the rain still pelting we settled into the DoC hut for a peaceful afternoon doze, and were starting to cook tea just on darkness when Tim Wallis dropped in.

He brought with him his Hughes 500 helicopter, teenage son and two mates, so to make room for them Dave, Sven and I shifted out of the DoC hut and into Beansprout's spare bedroom. It was beers all round, and Tim Wallis gave some chops to Beansprout and his wife. They fried them up immediately, and while his wife ate the meat, Beansprout very deliberately and with great satisfaction, ate all the fat.

Next morning it was still drizzling, but Tim took his lads down to the Hackett River for a shoot, then raced back and offered Beansprout

Beach stones near Barn Bay.

181

and Katherine a lift over to Wanaka 'for some shopping'! Seemed like
Tim had 'urgent business' to attend to over there. They gratefully ac-
cepted this opportunity, although the weather was getting thick and the
rain setting in. With a roar Tim and his passengers disappeared, while
we looked at the weather and decided on a 'pit' day—besides we wanted
to see how things were going to turn out. It did not look like flying
weather to us, but who were we to judge? (Incidentally, many years later
I was talking to David Elworthy of Shoal Bay Press, and it turned out
that he was the 'urgent business' and was sweltering in 35 degree heat in
Wanaka, waiting for Tim to turn up.)

By midday the storm had got heavier, and the radio said that
slips had closed the Haast highway. About one hour later the chopper returned with Tim and some well-shaken passengers. Katherine and
Beansprout looked pale, and Beansprout confessed that he'd never been
so alarmed, as Tim's repeated attempts to get over the Haast Pass were
blunted by heavy rain and zero visibility. At times they had just been
following the telephone wires barely five metres below them, ducking
and swerving along the curves of the road.

By now Tim began to feel he ought to be concerned about his boys
(remember them?) still mooching down at the Hackett River, so he
roared off again in his helicopter and was back an hour later with three
very drenched schoolboys.

After a feed at about four and some more jokes, Tim reckoned it
was clearing up, so off they went, barrelling up the West Coast highway.
They didn't return, so I guess they made it—we never heard otherwise.
We shifted back into the DoC hut, stoked up the fire, had a brew and
slowly allowed the wilderness to return. And this time, it did.

After that excitement the following day started drearily. Beansprout
rowed us across the tide-heavy Gorge Burn, and we had a wet trudge
to Barn Bay, slipping on the ankle-wrenching rocks. In places we could
still discern the line of boulders displaced by the trundling bulldozers
and their sledges from the mining company efforts in 1973. At the
Barn Bay hut a group of hunters sat morosely in a circle, staring at their

beers and grizzling about life. They did not seem to welcome three wet trampers so we moved on, following the four-wheel-drive track up the Cascade River.

This track got bulldozed again in 1977 when some entrepreneurs dragged out a huge nephrite boulder from near the mouth of the Cascade River. This exploit received a good deal of publicity in the newspapers at the time, though the story I later heard was that the greenstone turned out to be of an inferior grade. We squelched up the track, and as the nor'wester cleared away we found a pretty campsite beside some old podocarp forest. It was a serene, peaceful night, with no hint of wind, so it was all the more surprising that on the next day, when we arrived at the Cascade River, there were clear signs of a major windstorm.

Our anxiety at crossing a flooded Cascade River turned out to be groundless, but at the road end branches had been ripped off, trees tumbled over in the cow paddocks and iron ripped off the farm shed. When we tried to drive back there were dozens of trees blown all over the road. The first big one we managed to drive around, and we pulled another couple out of the way. One tree we attacked with our hammer and screwdrivers and managed to bend off sufficient branches to edge Mel underneath by a matter of half an inch, but finally our luck ran out. We got to a monster tree, and there was no way we were going to pull, cut or hack this beauty out of the way.

At that moment a car turned up on the far side; the driver took one look at the tree blocking his way and tootled back as fast as he could. How long would we have to wait before a guy with a chainsaw turned up? But Sven had an idea. To the left of the tree was a spaghnum moss swamp. What if we made a road of logs and rocks and drove around the tree? As the owner of the car likely to disappear in this mire, I dubiously inspected the solidity of the swamp as the others beavered away on their engineering project.

I didn't sink up to my neck in the ooze, it's true, but my body weight is a lot less than a Hillman Hunter's, and the whole swamp sucked and slathered as if eager for a meal of Mel. I pleaded with the guys, 'Let's not ruin a great trip eh?' But it was too late—they pronounced the 60 metres of 'road' (which was really two railway lines of rocks, branches and logs arranged in a hopeful parallel) ready for the test drive.

'Fast or slow?' I inquired sarcastically.

'Keep it medium.'

So I kept it medium and Mel made it—best damn car I ever had!

Stepping on a Million Stones

My tramping mate was always faster than me, because of longer or younger legs maybe, I never worked out which. I could never quite keep up and would find myself over-striding if I tried, so I usually eased off and plodded at my own pace while he disappeared down the valley track or the river bed. He never normally got more than 20 minutes ahead, and it was easier to let him go since I knew he'd wait for me somewhere. Still, it was uncanny at times how I would wander separately down the river bed, crossing apparently where I pleased, yet often come across a scuff mark or a rock still damp from a recent boot print. I was not deliberately trying to follow his trail, simply picking my own best way across the fords and over the boulders, but by some intuitive mechanism I invariably made the same choices as he had half an hour before.

When I looked back over the terrain it always seemed to me that our routes were pretty much the best ones: not the most direct or quickest necessarily, but a useful combination of easier travel over better fords, skirting the big boulders or awkward tangles of trees. In a game of chess, there is always the perfect move, the ideal play, and a computer can probably work it out given enough time, but most players do not have the time to work out all the combinations. Instead they pick a reasonable route through their opponent's defences, as we pick a reasonable route through a mountain's defences. For my mate and me, being economical was more crucial than picking the perfect line.

Trudging up to a pass near Mt Maitland in the Ohau Range: Kirsty Woods,
Sven Brabyn, Dale Parsons. (1989).

We always stopped for a brew and again, intuitively, would both select almost exactly the same place. We knew what we wanted: accessible dry firewood, close to a river, a good place for the fire, some views and rocks to bask against. I preferred sun, he liked a bit of shade. While he went for the big wood, I got the kindling, lit the fire and put the billy on, and when he returned with the larger stuff I stacked up the fire.

To an outsider it might look like a highly practised ritual, which it was. We both knew that the aim of the brew stop was to get the billy boiled as fast and as effortlessly as possible, then sit down and have a good rest and a chat afterwards. Jobs first, then relax. It rarely took longer than ten or fifteen minutes to boil the billy, throw in the tea and settle beside the fire for a snack. It is a gently combined effort, so that when both of you know what you're doing, want to achieve it in the shortest time and have done the task zillions of times before, it becomes effortless. It is like a Japanese tea ceremony in the New Zealand bush.

Logbook Entry, McCoy Hut
1 February 1989, Cooke, Wellington. Alpine traverse day 72 [sic].
It was a super day, so why not brew up on the Lyell Glacier after stepping on a million stones, and gaze at all the surroundings ...

David Cooke died on the Neish Glacier at the head of the Godley valley, on 8 February 1989. There is a memorial plaque to him at Aoraki/Mt Cook, and a line quoted from John Milton: "For solitude is sometimes best society."

We walk, we move, we leave behind a trail, a scent of living. The air shifts about us as we move forward and then slipstreams in our wake; our shadow swings this way and that, and it's impossible to enumerate how many insects we crush on the way into the forest, or how many we flush out as we pass by—but the fantails surely know. In India, believers of the Jain sect are so concerned at this accidental killing of insect life that they hold little brushes, which they use to flick before their feet. This is surely taking cause and effect to extremes, but it proves the point: that even in the simple locomotion of walking, humans leave a trail of ecological and historical debris.

Our feet make deep impressions or slight scuff marks. We stride with purpose or stumble aimlessly about without hope; but still we keep walking, because if we are not moving we must be asleep, or dead. We walk enough during our lifetimes to circumnavigate the world several times, or at least we used to.

The modern American mystic and guru Alan Watts once compared walking to a form of wakeful meditation, a patient and unglamorous way of cleansing the mind. Certainly when your stride hits the right rhythm, and your breathing is strong and your muscles tempered, there is a marvellous sense of both purpose and calm as you walk. You seem to extract the oxygen at an exhilarating rate, and the ceaseless change of location engages your senses in a sharp, unfuzzy way. Even as the muscles ache and the sweat dribbles unpleasantly into every corner of your body, when you do top the final rise, there is a wonderfully satisfying sense of gratification.

New Zealand is still a young country, with a difficult terrain that needs both tenacity and skill to navigate through. What is behind that mountain? Will there be a pass at the end of that river valley? This sense of questing has never been entirely absent from our culture, and the landscape is big enough and unknown enough to continue to satisfy that appetite.

People who visit Switzerland or Nepal are often struck by how many people live in the mountain environs, whereas in New Zealand the mountain landscape is mostly an empty one. The opportunities for adventure, solitude, companionship and life experiences in the hills have contributed substantially to the sort of national image that we like to see reflected in the mirror. Self-reliance, adaptability, toughness, endurance—these are qualities that run throughout the back-country traditions of New Zealand, whether they apply to gold-diggers and explorers, pioneer settlers, swaggers, high-country farmers or modern hunters and trampers.

Something in the mountains draws us to them, and it is striking how New Zealand (which has a coastline longer than Australia) has until recent years been a staunchly land-orientated culture. We have ignored the sea and focused our poetry and painting and wisdom into the back country. It has given us our heroes, our philosophers and our storytellers.

I continue to step on many stones and I have often asked myself: why do people go tramping? Belatedly, I have realised that writing this book is partly an attempt to answer that question.

For a start, people go tramping because the empty mountains are there, beckoning with tracks and huts and opportunities, a well-spring of adventure. It's the sport of 'Everyman', for anyone with legs and lungs could wander along the Abel Tasman coastal track or undertake one of the popular Great Walks. We often forget how many people in the world live in urban conglomerations where wilderness is something they see on the *Discovery* channel.

The mountains also offer an affordable, close-at-hand adventure. People can select a journey at their own level, from a family sojourn to a hard mountain epic, and the rewards are commensurate with the effort. Just like life, the more you put in, the more you get out.

Heading into the hills brings relief from cloying suburbs and work-place structures and strictures. It offers an opportunity to touch the natural elements of our life: to experience a river running, a chill blast of mountain air, the heat from an open fire and thick black nights cloaked in a profound silence. Tramping is also a timely reminder that our daily lives actually depend on natural, not human forces, and that in our ordinary lives we live on the crust of our environment, not in the environment itself.

Since people are increasingly agnostic in their daily lives, perhaps the experiences of the natural world offer a modest replacement for God. The wilderness humbles us, and sets a scale where, for once, we are not the dominant life-form, or even a life-form that will be around for very long. Mountains are millions of years old, and sometime in the future our little piece of dust will be compressed, heated and melded into another mountain again.

There are other reasons to go into the hills: the physical rewards of the exercise itself, the necessities of resourcefulness, the pleasure in risk, the social camaraderie of being with like-minded men and women. Is a view from a mountain ridge beautiful because few people have seen it, or is it beautiful because we have gained it by our effort and had the satisfaction of sharing that effort and view with friends?

I seem to be stating the obvious in trying to encapsulate the culture of tramping in a few paragraphs. It's a parallel life, known to those who have experienced it, neither better nor worse than the other lives we lead, but existing as a contrast. Some people live parallel lives as stock-car racers or surfers or artists, and sometimes these lives completely overwhelm their original life and become a self-fulfilling passion. Tramping at times has been like that for me, and I know that I have been fortunate.

If I have a wish it is to lead a slower life. Not one less rich or lacking in detail, but one concentrating on the quality of experience, rather than the quantity. It bemuses me that we have struggled for millennia to create an enormously complex civilisation just so that we can now sit and swill fizzy drinks while watching sport on satellite television. I have always been puzzled by politicians' speeches calling for increased economic growth in order to raise our standard of living, when it is glaringly obvious that most of us already enjoy a pretty high standard of life. I suspect that 'economic growth' and 'higher standard of living' are weaselly words for good old-fashioned greed.

Mountain air is a handy antidote to all this, but I once thought that tramping might become an old farts' pastime. It seemed during the 1990s that with the general pursuit of money and expansion of choice in recreational pursuits, the young bloods would not have enough time for the hills. But in Easter 2003 I was quite surprised at how many cars were parked at the road ends off the Arthur's Pass highway. It seemed that half of Christchurch was in the mountains, and glancing through the hut logbooks over the last couple of years there appear to be plenty of young Kiwis who are active trampers.

The lonely mountain valleys will always have their rightful place in New Zealand culture, and I'm pleased about that, for it means I'm not just talking to myself and a declining bunch of old fogey trampers. I'm talking to my child.

Rachel and I are both keen trampers, but for the moment we take smaller footsteps, following our skipping daughter along the tracks, her hair dancing in the wind. When she gets tired I lift her up on my shoulders, her weight being pleasantly like the two-week-tramp packs I used to lug about. I'm surprised to admit that being a father has been a greater pleasure than being a tramper, and I'm content to visit the mountains less often.

Anyway, I'm not sure how much longer I can get away with this tramping lark: someone is bound to tap me on the shoulder and remind me that I'm having too much fun and it's about time I got a proper job. But I can't see it happening. There are still too many valleys to wander up, and several more hut doorways to pause at, push back the bolt and let down the pack with a satisfying thump. Another great day done, time for a brew, eh?

Mark, Alex and Rachel.

Author's Note

Some years ago I had drawn up some private notes in a booklet on club tramping in the 1970s called *Tramping the Ranges*. It was never published and was written mainly because I did not want to forget those days myself, but it occurred to me that some of the observations might be of interest to present-day readers. Some things have changed drastically, others not at all. I extracted what I thought was of interest and included it in the section *Tongue and Meats*. Their website www.wtmc.org. nz is excellent.

At about the same time as I was researching the National Archives on another matter I came across a considerable number of tramping hut logbooks. Apparently their inclusion in the archives had been cause for some debate amongst archivists, but I was immensely grateful. The Department of Conservation inherited many old hut logbooks from the New Zealand Forest Service, but some of the original logbooks have disappeared, trashed in all probability. Nowadays DoC passes on its hut logbooks to the National Archives, and each regional branch holds logbooks from their area—for example, Christchurch Archives holds logbooks from Arthur's Pass and Aoraki/Mt Cook.

I usually found the best logbook entries in huts rather remote from the popular tramping trails, and usually in places where people can get stuck, like McCoy Hut on the Clyde River or St Winifreds Hut on the Havelock River. Fortunately, the Canterbury Mountaineering Club (CMC) have been thorough in saving their hut logbooks, which date back to the 1930s and include Park Morpeth Hut, St Winifreds Hut,

Havelock Hut and many others. These are now kept in the Canterbury Museum library.

Anyone who has read this far will have realised that I have more than a passing interest in back-country history and under the guise of story-telling have snuck in all sorts of irrelevancies. My information on mustering gangs in the section *Home on the Range* comes from my father-in-law, Stephen Barker, who mustered and acted as a packie into Sutherlands Hut on Four Peaks Station in the 1940s, as well as mustering on Erewhon and other stations. A good deal of my Tararua history has been gleaned from Chris Maclean's excellent book *Tararua*.

My information on Sergeant Garvey came from two sources, *The Mt Ida Goldfields: a Merchant's Memories* (1988) by J. G. Bremner, originally published in the *Mt Ida Chronicle* in 1911. Bremner managed a store on the goldfield and knew many of the participants, and gives a detailed description of the incident. *Early Days in Central Otago* (1930) by Robert Gilkison was my other source, though it is both inaccurate and unreliable. For people interested in Whacka Anderson of Patriarch Station, there is one sound recording of him that can be obtained through Radio New Zealand archives. He is a remarkable storyteller and is also featured in *More Grady's People* by Don Grady.

For more interesting history on the swaggers see *Roughnecks, Rolling Stones and Rouseabouts* and *Shining with the Shiner*, both by John A. Lee; and for John the Baptist and Freddie Ambrose see Mona Anderson's *The Good Logs of Algidus*. My information on the mining episodes in South Westland's Red Hills comes from a 1977 Federated Mountain Clubs publication *Red Mountain—National Park or Asbestos Mine?* by Les Molloy.

The history of deer-culling in New Zealand is complex, and I only attempt to briefly sketch out the period. *Shooting for the Skipper* (1971) by Jack McNair gives a good flavour of deer-culling in the 1930s under Captain Yerex, and I would also recommend *Pack & Rifle* (1995 edition) by Philip Holden and *Sock in My Stew: memories of Dick Morris and the deer cullers* (1991) by Robin S. Patterson.

I have used metric units rather than imperial, except for historical references, though most of my generation straddled both sorts of measurements and we coped somehow. Phrases such as 'they slogged along for miles', or 'we were inching closer', have connotations for me that simply cannot be rendered in a metric version with any sort of poetry.

Before writing this book I investigated what had been written before. I read a large number of tramping club journals from North and South Island clubs and also dipped into the somewhat meagre collection of published books on tramping stories. Most are as ancient as the hills themselves. *Peaks, Packs and Mountain Tracks* (1940) by W. Scott Gilkison is an early attempt to tell tramping and mountaineering stories. John Pascoe's two books, *Unclimbed New Zealand* (1939) and *Land Uplifted High* (1952), are a mix of tramping and mountaineering, as are Paul Powell's two books, *Men Aspiring* (1967) and *Just where do you think you've been?* (1970). Powell writes vividly and candidly, and his books deserve to be reprinted. The classic book on Fiordland exploration *Beyond the Southern Lakes: the explorations of W. G. Grave* (1950) has some marvellous epics of bush-bashing and has quite rightly been reprinted.

In the last 30 years, as far as I can judge, there have been no books devoted exclusively to tramping stories published. *Classic Walks* (1997) by Craig Potton, *Classic Tramping in New Zealand* (1999) by Shaun Barnett and Rob Brown, and *True South* (2003) by Pat Barrett have story-telling elements, but are still in effect guidebooks. *Waking to the Hills* (1985) by Geoff Spearpoint is similar in style to my own *The Hills* (1988), both being generalised descriptions of tramping culture.

Aat Vervoorn's two autobiographies are worth a look, though they are based more on climbing ascents. *Beyond the Snowline* (1981) and *Mountain Solitudes* (2000) attempt a different type of story-telling from what has been usual in New Zealand mountain literature. The stories are both introspective and philosophical, and I must admit to being quite baffled at times by some of the more elevated passages. In some measure both Powell's and Vervoorn's books helped me to adjust the tone for my own writing.

It surprised me when I started to write these tramping stories just how many I had to leave out. There is a wealth of material about the hills, and when you sit around with a group of friends in a mountain hut the stories come pouring out—serious, tragic, comical and thoughtful. The world of tramping has still barely been touched on.

Acknowledgements

Firstly, great thanks to the people who provided their own stories: Penny Hazard ('Garden of Eden' and 'Lake Grave') and Kirsty Woods ('Avalanche!'). Thanks to Philip Holden for permission to reproduce the extract from *Pack and Rifle*, and also to Jonathan Jull for allowing his after-avalanche image to be published (the photo was taken by Kirsty Woods). Apologies to Mark Brabyn who provided a great story which I never used, mainly because I couldn't find the right place for it. As I began to tell my own stories I became attuned to other people's storytelling abilities, and my thanks go to John Madgwick in particular, who inspired a number of ideas which I developed for this book.

Several people read my draft text and made observations and comments, so thanks are due to Rachel Barker, Nic Bishop, Sven Brabyn, Penny Hazard, John Madgwick and Geoff Spearpoint. Geoff also allowed me to access his huge collection of tramping club journals and tramping books.

I'm grateful to Mike Hollis for allowing me to reproduce some of his photos, and to both Mike and Hugh Middleton for filling in some gaps and confirming, at least in part, the accuracy of my memory.

Appreciation also goes out to Arnold Heine for some heritage hut history.

Alexandra (my five-year-old daughter) suggested a few titles for the book when I was grappling with the problem, which included the loyal 'My Dad, the Tramper', the ambiguous 'Tramping Can be Fun', or the accurate 'I Get Smelly When I go Tramping'.

It is customary to state here that all mistakes and inaccuracies are my own, which of course they are. But when other people have shared your experiences and can provide counter-evidence or embellishments to your story, I now understand the truth of the saying that a creative work is never finished, only abandoned.

I would finally like to thank the many special tramping friends with whom I have shared many experiences, blunders and glorious moments over the years—in alphabetical order:

Rachel Barker, Nic Bishop, Sven Brabyn, Barbara Brown, Ian Bunckenburg, Mary Elmers, Bernie Frankpitt, Dave Glenny, Tom Halliburton, Mike Hollis, Alan Hooker, Paul Hughes, Paula Kibblewhite, Nick Miller, Jan Simmons, Geoff Spearpoint and Kirsty Woods.